Transforming Supervision in Health Care

Also available from Cassell:

Evans: *Supervisory Management*

Farrant: *Sibling Bereavement*

Forsyth: *Career Skills*

Goddard: *Informative Writing*

Maitland: *Recruiting*

Osborne: *Staff Training and Assessment*

Roberts: *Dismissal*

Wilmot: *The Ethics of Community Care*

Transforming Supervision in Health Care

DON MASON

CASSELL

London and New York

Cassell

Wellington House
125 Strand
London WC2R 0BB

370 Lexington Avenue
New York
NY 10017-6550

First published 1999

British Library Cataloguing-in-Publication Data
A catalogue record for this book is available from the British Library.

ISBN 0-304-70463-6 (paperback)

Typeset by ensystems Ltd, Saffron Walden
Printed and bound in Great Britain by Biddles Ltd,
Guildford and King's Lynn

Contents

CHAPTER 1

Background

What this book is about

This is a practical book dealing with the design and implementation of a management development programme for supervisory and junior middle managers. It covers all phases of the process, from its inception to the evaluation of the outcomes of the programme.

It describes how the initial concept was refined and elaborated by trainers and management colleagues into a learning system tailored to meet the personal and organizational needs of those affected by it. The idea was fully validated in discussion with managers at all levels, from the chief executive to the supervisors who were the target audience. This period of consultation was an essential part of the marketing of the training programme.

The account also details the methods used to enable participants on the programme to change their management behaviour and bring about associated improvements in organizational performance.

A practical model for management development

The approach to management development outlined here has gained a track record for meeting the needs of supervisors in a growing number of health service organizations. It evolved as a response to the changes brought about in one of the numerous reorganizations experienced in the British National Health Service (NHS), and has continued to be tested in successive changes that have beset the service.

This book is based on the experience of NHS trainers who set out to change the way supervisors were developed, and did so in full partnership with line managers at all levels in the organization. This partnership provided trainers and managers alike with the opportunity to build a mutually supportive approach to the pressing problem of improving how management and leadership operate at the front line. By working together, they sowed the seeds of a continuing symbiotic relationship between those responsible for organizational development and their colleagues responsible for organizational performance. This joint relationship between line managers and trainers adds to the contribution that each of their functions makes to the total performance of managers, and gives useful insights into what can be achieved when trainers and managers work together.

The success of the approach may be judged by the degree of support that has been given to it by senior managers. This is especially so at the executive level, where directors have followed the development of supervisors closely and have demonstrated their support through participation in tutorials and in the award ceremonies at which successful candidates receive their certificates.

Managers as trainers

Senior managers who nominate their supervisors to the programme also act as sponsors in a more practical way by being mentors and coaches to candidates throughout the programme. This is a valuable and valued involvement because it engages senior managers as an integral part of the total training resource and ensures that the training remains closely connected with the operational reality of the workplace.

It has the additional benefit of bringing manager and supervisor together in a partnership for mutual learning that continues after the supervisor has completed the programme. By its example, the partnership provides a driving force for changing attitudes to training and development, and it will be seen later how this can be used to create a learning environment in the workplace.

The main benefit of the collaboration between trainers and managers is found in the achievements of those who have followed the programme. Not only is there a measurable improvement in the management knowledge and skills of individuals but they become better team players by working together on the team problem-solving exercise, which is the most important learning opportunity in the programme.

Learning by doing

The team problem-solving project is where the theory of management learned in the programme is applied to achieve practical operational results for the organization. It has been said that 'theory without practice is sterile'. This stage of the learning programme integrates theory with practice in a dynamic way to achieve fruitful and productive results.

The programme aims to help supervisors learn new management skills, or refresh their understanding of old ones. By concentrating on the skills that supervisors themselves know will make them more effective, the programme keeps focused on the practicalities of managing in the organization. This approach avoids the trap of continually seeking to import the latest management techniques into the curriculum.

In practical terms, the old, time-tested tools are often the best for dealing with old, time-tested problems. They may not be as trendy as some of the flavour-of-the-month management techniques that come with monotonous regularity onto an already saturated market. But many of the old methods have the merit of actually achieving results and, by using these techniques in this development programme, it has been possible to give people the skills they need to make them work even more effectively.

Trainers who are responsible for designing management development programmes of this kind will have many opportunities to enhance their own professional development. Ideally, the learning curves of trainers and programme participants will follow a parallel course, for both groups learn in the mutually supportive relationship that is built into the programme.

Shared rewards

The rewards of effective learning are also shared. Supervisors learn to lead effectively, to solve problems, decide on courses of action, to communicate, motivate their teams and achieve goals. Their reward is found in their increased confidence, self-esteem, and ability to get results from the resources at their disposal, and especially in getting results from their teams.

Trainers, on the other hand, get satisfaction from planning and leading the learning process, acting as the yeast in the leaven, and helping trainees to take responsibility for helping themselves to change first their paradigms, then their behaviours. Training and development is a prime example of a win–win situation and should be approached with that outcome in mind.

Trainers and managers together

This book is primarily for trainers who are faced with the continuing challenge of having to come up with effective methods of developing managers at the front line of their organizations. The approach outlined here has a wide application beyond the NHS environment in which it was first conceived. It will also be of interest to line managers. Their involvement in the training and development role is gradually being recognized, but this still needs to be given greater recognition and prominence as part of the manager's responsibility towards people.

CHAPTER 2

Strategy

There is no doubt that management development has increased in UK organizations over the past ten or fifteen years. In 1997, the Open Business School report *Portrait of Management Development* found that the 'vast majority of firms are training'.

Whereas in 1986 the average number of formal training days per manager had been 3.1 days a year, this had risen to 5.5 days by 1996, and was predicted to rise to 7.3 days in the future. The question, however, is not how much training is being done, but how effective is it?

Most organizations still do not have a policy statement on management development, nor a special budget for it. This points both to a lack of commitment at the top and to the arbitrary nature of the approach made by these organizations to the development of their human capital.

Organizations may argue that they prefer to fund the development of their managers out of the overall training budget set aside for all the training needs envisaged throughout the organization, but this can mean that there is no clear idea of what is being spent specifically on management development. The reality often is that managers are not developed according to any planned system that has been prepared to ensure the organization's long-term strategic advantage.

It is also likely that organizations will develop their managers in the 'sink or swim' school of management survival, expecting their managers to learn to manage by doing it, as though the skill and art of management are somehow instilled when the manager is promoted. Supervisory managers are especially prone to this treatment.

This approach continues to be supported by many senior managers who are alumni of the university of life, and although their numbers are waning they can still adversely influence the way management development is perceived in their organizations. If senior managers believe that their own management development gained by this arbitrary trial and error method was good enough for them, they may not support changes in the way their first-line and junior middle managers learn to become effective.

The management development gap

There are still many gaps between the organizational need to develop managers and an actual commitment to designing and delivering an effective training and development system to support them in their jobs. That this is so is shown in research undertaken by the Institute of Science and Technology of Manchester University, based on five years of tracking the pressures faced by managers.

The report *The Quality of Working Life*, published in 1998, showed that 64 per cent of managers feel under constant time pressure and 65 per cent are struggling to find a balance between their home and work lives. Increasingly, these are symptoms pointing to low motivation, job insecurity and the erosion of performance. Managers are floundering because they are ill equipped to cope with the changes that are shaping their roles and responsibilities.

Managers need to develop the capability to deal with change if they are to direct their efforts whole-heartedly to the survival of the organization and not spend most of their energy on ensuring the survival of themselves. Organizations need to pay more attention to management development, not less.

Change and evolution

All organizations undergo change: it is a natural part of the evolutionary process that affects all our institutions, whether in the private or public sectors. But, in the public sector, the NHS is probably the most visible example of an organization affected by incessant change on a massive scale, and it is the cumulative effects of pressures brought about by change and the continual efforts to cope with its many manifestations that have had so damaging an effect on morale, especially amongst managers. Perhaps the time has come to consider how this situation might be improved and to tackle the malaise by giving managers better training, better support and better tools to do their jobs.

The urgency of the need becomes apparent when we consider the climate in which organizations operate. If the socio-economic environment is a battlefield where organizations are fighting for survival, then the NHS would be classified as the walking wounded. It is in urgent need of drastic treatment but has to soldier on without relief because there are no reinforcements to carry on its work. To continue the metaphor, the NHS has had its fill of traditional medicine, whether this is practised as surgery, resulting in the repeated amputation of structures and services, or by implanting newly reconstituted systems and procedures, or in blood transfusions of billions of pounds of public money. Perhaps the time is approaching when we have to say 'Physician, heal thyself!', and trust that the NHS will try some forms of alternative medicine on itself.

The thought is not as fanciful as it may appear at first sight. Most breakthroughs in health care come about through trial and error, by continuing research and the application of the results that are found to work in removing the underlying problem. Improving the functioning of NHS managers should follow a similar process of care. The difference is that management trainers are both the diagnosticians and the doctors in the case. But it is perfectly possible for them to apply the traditional health treatment model to managers who are expecting trainers to help them to improve their fitness to carry out their work.

Developing managers from within the organization so they can ensure that the public is served effectively at the point of their need seems to be a matter for determination by the local health care organization. It does not need to await the launch of a major national initiative.

The issue of improving managers is a local one, capable of being recognized, diagnosed and treated on the spot. Yet, when in-house training and development is carried out, it is often seen to be inadequate by those at the receiving end, with many current management development initiatives being held in low esteem even by the employers initiating them, according to some recent research from the Cranfield University School of Management by Sally Atkinson and Mike Meldrum. They report in *The Management Development Gap* (1998) that when senior and middle managers were asked to rate the quality of the management in their organizations, 73 per cent rated it average or below, and 79 per cent believed it was not meeting the needs of the business. Ninety per cent, however, thought management development could play a more significant role in advancing the aims of the organization.

There is every reason to believe that this thinking is shared by senior managers in the NHS. An underlying unease that in-house management development will not meet the needs of their managers may be a reason why so much management training in the NHS is bought in from external providers, or else managers (especially those at the top level) are sent on courses. The reservations about the quality of in-house training may even account for the general lack of commitment in NHS organizations to developing their employees in line with the Investors in People standards. The low level of attainment of this national benchmark for effective training and development of employees strongly suggests that many of the component organizations in the NHS which could qualify are failing to measure their attainments in the development of people against national yardsticks. Whatever the reasons may be for this apparent reluctance to develop their own managers, the solution lies in the hands of trainers.

Better management, better customer care

This book is about how to build better management in health and social care. These sectors of the public service have a constant impact on the well-being of people. Their objective is to deliver effective care to help people gain and maintain good physical and mental health. The National Health Service, social services and their partner organizations in the private care industry all have to manage and deliver health care to the nation. This may ultimately prove to be an insuperable task, since the demand for health care seems destined to outweigh the availability of resources to satisfy it. But it is in the nature of people to strive to protect themselves, to seek for safety and security, and to overcome barriers placed in the way of survival.

It is human nature for individuals to marshal their resources to fight the diseases that afflict them. Organizations are only groups of individuals brought together to pursue a common purpose. They attain their common purposes by providing effective management to co-ordinate and control their resources. Organizations do not survive unless they are managed effectively, nor do they last long if they fail to ensure that managers are developed to cope with changing circumstances.

The management of the NHS is under continual pressure to provide effective health care. Good management is an indispensable function in all organizations, but is especially necessary in an organization as complex as the NHS if resources – particularly the human resource – are to produce the results that are intended.

Management provides the strategic direction for people to follow as they fulfil the organization's purpose. Organizational values and mission, and the procedural, financial and human systems through which the care is delivered are all part of the management ethos and need to be communicated and understood by all who deliver their specialized services to patients and clients. The equation is simply put: high-quality people equal high-quality health care. This analogy applies equally well to any other organization – simply substitute 'performance' for 'health care' in the last sentence.

Developing tomorrow's managers

In this book we will discuss the theme of management development, with particular reference to developing supervisory or front-
line managers, who are responsible for the delivery of the
organization's purposes to the public. But management development has to be inclusive. Over four decades ago, Peter Drucker
wrote: 'In fine, management development must embrace all managers in the enterprise. It must aim at challenging all to growth
and self-development. It must focus on performance rather than
promise, and tomorrow's requirements rather than those of
today.'

We will explain how a strategy to improve the calibre of
supervisory managers was conceived, planned, implemented and
evaluated in a health care organization through a development
programme designed to be responsive to organizational and
individual needs. This strategy provided the drive to extend
management development throughout the organization.

The programme aimed to test the contention that managers of
tomorrow can be made in an organization. It challenged the way
supervisors had been trained in the organization up to that time
by rethinking the purpose, process and pay-off of a new approach.

Although the strategy began with supervisors, it quickly
expanded to meet the development needs of more senior managers and of many employees who aspired to enter management.
The result was a transformation in the way supervisors and other
managers were developed which opened up new opportunities
for trainers to form a learning partnership of great significance
and lasting effectiveness.

By this means the organization was able to improve the capability of its managers. This is an objective sought, and achieved with
varying degrees of success and urgency, wherever the phrase
'better management, better health' is taken seriously.

Focusing on the supervisor

The purpose of the book is to provide an account of how first-line managers have been developed to operate more effectively as the leaders of their teams in care organizations. Supervisors are important because they manage the interface between the organization and its customers. In the case of the NHS, it is first-line supervisors who have a major influence on the quality of the service delivered to patients and clients – the customers for care. It is here that the service provider succeeds or fails in the eyes of the client. More effort, not less, needs to be given to the way supervisors are developed if they are to be effective custodians of the organization's future.

To develop supervisors to lead their teams with insight and understanding, take responsibility for the further development of their teams and bring out the hidden potential of themselves and their people, is a challenging objective for any organization. In the following pages we show how it was achieved in one health authority, and offer this as an approach which others may adopt and adapt to their particular needs.

This development programme has already been modified to fit the needs of many other health care providers, and it is hoped that some of its ideas and approaches will be a spur for further emulation. After all, ideas should be used as springboards and progress is nearly always made by starting with past experience and building anew on that foundation. What was plagiarism is now called benchmarking, and benchmarking (we are all assured) is the route to continuous improvement.

Responding to change

The programme was conceived to meet the needs of an organization coming to terms with change on an unprecedented scale. Within three years of its inception the programme had been recognized by its winning a National Training Award and the Award for Excellence given by the Institute for Supervision and Management. Whilst these were important in setting a seal of approval, the most valuable outcome of the programme was provided by the supervisors and managers who went through it, and who were transformed in the process in ways which they will know and others will recognize.

CHAPTER 3

Internal partnerships

Why develop supervisors?

There are many reasons to improve the way supervisory development is carried out in an organization. Perhaps the old systems of training have become outmoded and need to be replaced with more up-to-date techniques. The use of open learning systems, computer-based training and the recent emphasis on continuing professional development through self-managed learning are cases in point. Maybe supervisory development has been contracted out to external providers who fail to keep abreast of the changes constantly affecting the organization, and so provide training in how to deal with change that is not grounded in reality. By accident or design, organizations can lose their grip on management development by abrogating this role to external providers. This is not to say that outside providers do not have a part to play in management development. They do, but they should complement, and not replace, the organization's own training function.

The organization needs to be much more closely involved in the development process, and be seen to be committed to its success. The priority is to build dedicated and effective managers from within, supported in their development by the organization and reflecting its ethos and values in a way that no outsider can do. The objective is to build managers who are absolutely clear about the organization's purpose, are convinced of its values, and who, by their example, can lead others to deliver the goods and services required. If the organization is to give exceptional service, then a management development programme is a principal pre-requisite to enable managers to lead others to that goal.

Organizations tend to respond to change by default. They react to influences from the environment in which they operate, but seldom make it a practice to design and implement specific innovations to deal with changes which they could have foreseen through effective strategic planning. Strategic planning can ident-ify the threat, and may determine what needs to be done about it, but setting priorities and taking action to deal with them are real-time activities which cannot be left to manage themselves.

The outcome is that the planning cycle produces fire-fighting activities, not fire-prevention ones. The difference is to concen-trate on reactivity, not pro-activity, and changes that in hindsight should have been initiated by the organization are delayed until some external pressure makes it no longer possible to carry on in the old way.

Change is the spur

The spur to change a management development programme often follows this pattern. In the case we will describe in this account, the impetus to change the way managers were developed came from a national perception that the NHS was under-per-forming and its resources – not only financial but human also – were not being managed to gain the greatest value for the greater number of their clients. Basic management concepts and tech-niques were inadequately understood, and there was a reluctance to adopt management systems that were used successfully in major organizations in the private sector.

Added to this, the NHS had also become highly bureaucratic and departmentalized so that diverse functions failed to co-operate and combine effectively to apply their special capabilities and expertise to patients and clients. In a word, the NHS needed new leadership, and it was this realization that led it to introduce general management in the early 1980s.

NHS management review

The government had set up a management review of the NHS headed by Roy (later Sir Roy) Griffiths, a businessman from a major supermarket chain. The review findings were embodied in a letter to the Prime Minister of the day which said, in effect, NHS management has been reviewed and found wanting. The Report chairman made a telling observation on the diffuse management structure of the service. He reflected that Florence Nightingale, had she searched the corridors of NHS power with her lamp, would have been as hard pressed as he was to find who was in charge.

This was a reflection on the then prevalent style of consensus management, which required top-level decision-making to be a responsibility shared by a management team of diverse professionals. These included members of the medical and nursing professions, together with an administrator and a treasurer. This arrangement might appear to have been democratic, and gave the impression that decision-making power was shared, but it blurred the line of accountability.

Changing the management ethos

The review recommended that the NHS adopt the structure of general management prevailing in most other large organizations. There was also the need to improve understanding of basic management concepts and techniques and apply them to the way the NHS was run. The Griffiths Report, published in 1983 as *The NHS Management Inquiry*, heralded a radical new way of managing health services in the UK.

Looking back with the perspective of time, it is difficult now to realize the impact that this Report and its recommendations had on the NHS and its decision-makers. In effect, the significant change was to be the establishment of one general manager at the highest level of all management units of the NHS who would have overall accountability for the achievement of planned performance. This major organizational change had repercussions throughout the NHS and exposed an immediate need for management awareness and skills to be developed in all functions, including medical and nursing services.

New management needs new managers

The introduction of general management caused all health authorities to reappraise their attitude to management and to see what should be done to improve the development of managers at all levels. It provided the spur for one health authority to take its management development programme seriously and build on opportunities to provide comprehensive in-house support to its managers.

In taking this approach forward, the authority's training function was able to play an influential part in developing managers so that they could gain organizational goals more effectively. This development also had the parallel strategy of helping them to identify and attain their personal goals through the application of self-development.

We believe this is a form of complementary achievement that can best be managed within an organization and in a context where the interdependence of self-development and organizational development is immediately apparent. In-house development means helping the manager to attain qualities and competences which can be applied to the attainment of the organizational goals.

Symbiotic management development

Management development is a symbiotic relationship, in which both the manager and the organization are able to grow, and this account of how that relationship can be developed affords many insights into a management development process that has proved its effectiveness in health care situations.

The spur to redesign a management development programme can come from many sources, but often an innovation comes as a response to change. Changes in the environment in which the organization operates are constantly arising, and each will need to be handled by prepared managers. In helping their own managers to deal with change, the organization is giving them the tools to face an uncertain future. It was environmental change on a major scale that led to the review of supervisory development described here.

Evolutionary change, revolutionary pace

Although the impetus that prompted one health authority to embark on this radical rethink of its training philosophy was imposed by a revolution in the way it was to be managed, there are other causes of change that need to be responded to on a daily basis. The pace of change in the world in general, and in industry and commerce and public services in particular, is increasing rapidly and exponentially. The management of change is the constant preoccupation of managers. Perceptive organizations have to take steps to enable their managers to deal with the turbulence of change – what Charles Handy has termed 'endless white water' – if they are to keep afloat.

In our NHS example, the turbulence caused by the introduction of new management structures, relationships and processes meant that every level of management had to respond to a new set of circumstances and start acting in different ways. The training task for the training function was immense and seemingly overwhelming and would have remained so if trainers had tried to respond to the total challenge. The way forward had to be to take one step at a time.

It was decided that efforts would be concentrated first on designing a programme for first-line managers, but to keep in mind the intention to expand this to the rest of management over time.

The importance of first-line management

First-line managers were selected as the starting-point for the new management development strategy for several reasons. They are the implementers of the corporate purpose, putting into effect the organizational directives that are planned and authorised at higher levels. In times of major organizational change they have to assume greater responsibilities from their senior managers, who are themselves involved in formulating the organization's new strategic direction in response to the change.

Again, supervisors comprise by far the largest proportion of the total management team. Arguably, they have the greatest influence on the way the workforce carries out its duties, on motivation, and on communication of the organization's intent and purpose to employees. In all of these areas, they are unlikely to be as skilled as they should be. Consequently, any development programme that concentrates its efforts onto this group of managers and helps them to achieve better results is likely to multiply its effectiveness by leveraging the benefits of training into the workplace.

Training supervisors helps them to fit more effectively into the management structure. Often, their role is understated and given scant recognition. For the most part they are poorly trained. Rarely is there a sustained attempt to break out of this pattern, yet opportunities to do so exist all the time, because change is always with us and better management of change will always be the primary management task.

Supervisors as creative leaders

Moreover, training supervisors to play a more creative role in the way they exercise leadership gives them the skill to help their teams to tackle day-to-day problems as they arise. Rather than being reactive in the face of challenges, a creative supervisor will be pro-active and more self-reliant. They will be confident and have the courage to do what is necessary without constantly referring upwards for permission.

Organizations that provide opportunities for their supervisors to gain the skills, behaviours and new mind-sets to fit them to cope with the changes that will continue to impact on the organization send a clear message that they mean their supervisors to be the best they can be. The message is that people are capable of more than they realize, and it is the purpose of training and development to release this latent potential for the benefit of all concerned.

What steps can be taken to revive inadequate supervisory development, or even to introduce it where it is not being practised? There are many roads and no right or wrong directions. The one we consider in this account has the advantage that it has passed the test of time and has been validated by thousands of managers who have followed it. This is not to say that it sprang into life fully formed. Although the initial concept has remained remarkably firm and inviolate, the implementation of the idea has been continually improved in response to feedback. New ideas and best management practice have been continually introduced to keep it up to date, based on the changing roles that supervisors have told us they need to enact.

Over the years, it has been found to offer a useful mix of experiences that have been valued by practising supervisors working in the health care sector of public service. It has been enthusiastically supported by top management. Above all, it has proved to be of practical benefit to supervisors and has given support to the argument that the development of managers benefits both managers and the organization.

There is a continuing demand for a step-by-step description of what it takes to make supervisory management development a reality. That it was introduced into a health care organization does not mean that it only has relevance in that setting. The principles and practice can be adapted to an extensive range of settings, for it will be seen that the methods are simple to understand, easy to apply, and focused on results for the individual and for the organization.

This is a case study of what has been done, and what has been done can be done again. Helping supervisors to excel will bring valuable benefits to any organization. Experiment with the steps described here. Modify them to fit your organization. Use the blueprint to build your own management development programmes. Energy and enthusiasm will be needed. So will patience and commitment. But results are there to be achieved, and their value will far outweigh the effort put in to gain them.

CHAPTER 4

Planning

First things first

Whether starting a supervisory programme from scratch or changing an existing one, the first step is to decide where to begin. This is not as banal as it sounds. Stephen Covey, author of *The Seven Habits of Highly Effective People* and, with Roger Merrill, of *First Things First*, has a simple response that can prompt action. 'Start with the end in mind' is his advice. It leads directly to visualizing the shape and scope of the end-product. Contemplating what the programme will be like when it is finally operating may seem to be an exercise in crystal-ball gazing, but it is as well to remember that a major barrier to achievement is the lack of a clear purpose. Time spent in creating the vision of what you want to achieve is seldom wasted.

Plan for success

Planning is essential for success. The scale of the cultural and operational changes required to introduce effective supervisory development programmes is often overwhelming to those who contemplate it. The task can seem so daunting that the easy way out is not to get involved at all. This is the frame of mind that condemns many projects to perish before they see the light of day. It is often prevalent in large, complex organizations glued together by diverse multi-functional professional layers of bureaucracy. Here, the difficulty of bringing new ideas to fruition has been likened to wading through treacle.

The NHS is an example of such an organization. Even the units of management known as NHS Trusts mirror all the complexities of the health service as a whole, and this complexity will pose a challenge to those planning to establish new management development arrangements. But it is at local level, at or near the patients and clients, that the need for effective management of care is most apparent. It is there that the public can recognize the quality of management in the quality of the service they receive. Consequently, the need for effective management development arrangements are especially important at the local level.

The need for professional integration

The NHS delivers its care through interconnecting professional structures that are not confined to the traditional disciplines of medicine, nursing and the professions allied to care. There are also the many support services, of which administration, finance, ambulance, works and maintenance departments, stores and supply functions, and contracting and commissioning functions are examples. All of these have special professional development needs to be satisfied to enable them to perform their duties.

Most of the professional skills associated with these functions are taught in the various specialized training programmes, which initially often last for many years. Many professions require regular refresher training to preserve the right of their members to continue in practice. During this professional training some areas of general management may be touched on, but these are not normally treated in any great depth. This has the effect of diminishing the importance of management in the eyes of many professionals in health care. Doctors, in particular, and, to a lesser extent, nursing professionals still retain a somewhat jaundiced view of the value of management.

Management development for professionals

The purpose of management development programmes is to redress this imbalance and graft onto professional service practitioners a sense that management too is a profession and to give them a deeper understanding of the basics that are needed to run the organization as a goal-seeking entity. Care professionals in the NHS who are trained in aspects of general management are better able to support the general management ethos within which the NHS operates.

Professional training enables each speciality to deliver its part of the care contract to patients. It also builds up an identity and *esprit de corps* within the profession but which, however, can lead to isolation and demarcation. In health care, as in social services and other like organizations, many working groups must combine their specialized contributions to make up the total package of care. This entails teamworking of an advanced order, which is all the more difficult to attain because of the demarcation that exists between the functions.

Breaching departmental boundaries

The need to penetrate these invisible but none the less real boundaries between functions is an essential management development objective, and the supervisory development programme should be planned to accentuate interdependence and demonstrate how teamworking can be achieved in practice.

One of the outcomes of the supervisory management development programme will be to enable participants to break out of their limiting behaviours. Professional isolationism is one such limitation that impairs effective communication and co-operation between the professions. This is an example of a behaviour which adversely affects the way that departments interact and co-operate. The training function has to act in such a way as to help managers to recognize that co-operation is preferable to confrontation, and that partnership improves productivity.

The chemistry of co-operation

Creating the conditions in which teams can work together effectively is like producing a chemical reaction under laboratory
conditions. In the laboratory, the purpose is to combine elements
to yield a different result. You take the elements from their
bottles, mix them into a retort, add a catalyst, and heat with a
Bunsen burner. The individual elements combine, and distil off
as a new product.

Our supervisory development programme mirrors this
sequence by bringing together team members from many different disciplines to achieve a common end-result. They are the
chemicals: where they carry out their work is the retort, and the
heat is the energy they apply to achieve their goal of effective
joint working. But, just as the chemical experiment needed a
catalyst to induce the change, so the teamworking experience will
be enhanced by the action of a facilitator, someone from outside
the team who helps the team to reach its goal, normally the
trainer involved in the development programme.

Catalysts

Other catalysts are also at work. Values, shared understanding,
and clarity of purpose are catalysts. So are morale and team spirit,
commitment, and a focus on results. All of these factors will be
instilled into supervisors in a well-planned development programme. In itself the programme is an experiment in organizational chemistry, with the catalytic role undertaken by the
programme leaders acting as facilitators, and the end-product of
the experiment being a cohort of supervisors with new skills and
the motivation and confidence to apply them with enthusiasm
and judgment.

The logical extension of this idea led to the introduction of
formal teambuilding sessions into the development programme,
to enable groups from different backgrounds to share their
experience to solve practical problems together. By using a set of
simple principles about the purpose and aims of teamworking it

was possible to establish a team-based training strategy that appealed to managers, supervisors and trainers. The catalyst was provided by trainers who acted as facilitators throughout the programme. This concept of shared learning became the foundation of all the in-house training that was subsequently introduced into the organization.

The process of enabling managers to use their combined experience to resolve problems which they have a mutual interest in overcoming is known as action learning. The concept and application of action learning to management development will be covered in depth in a later chapter. It will be seen to form an integral part of the philosophy and practice of this supervisory development programme, and is the basis for the final project work phase of the training where learning is put into practical effect.

Identifying stakeholders and planning consultation strategies

Within the planning stage of the programme we need to consider all those who will be involved, either as participants or as supporters of the programme. Many people play different roles in the production of the programme. They are all stakeholders, interested to different degrees in its success. Programme developers should be aware of who they are, and why and how to involve them in the design of the training.

Preliminary discussions on the proposed programme need to be set up with key people. Taking soundings in face-to-face discussions with as many individuals and groups as possible is an important way of communicating the intentions of the programme to others. It also helps the trainer to identify those who will support and those who will oppose the development. This is important basic market research, which needs to be taken into account so that ways around likely opposition can be planned in advance. Often, the best way of getting a change accepted is to identify those who support it and enlist them in planning and implementing the necessary actions. It is important to achieve visible and effective results quickly so that the momentum of

progress can be seen. It will not be long before many of the
hitherto uncommitted will stop dragging their feet and become
associates of success.

Stakeholders

1 Top management

Stakeholders provide the trainer with a wide range of contacts
from inside and outside the organization. First amongst them are
the top management team and the executive directors. They must
be cultivated carefully throughout the planning stage so that they
are clear about the intentions of the programme and can understand the importance of being seen to be involved as champions
of the development strategy.

2 Supervisors

The supervisory management team at whom the programme is
aimed will naturally be important stakeholders. This category
should also include those who may be termed aspiring supervisors. These are the up and coming employees with career
aspirations to become supervisors and who will be interested in
entering the development programme when it has been established. They will provide a large reservoir from which to draw the
organization's future managers.

3 Trainers

Obviously, the members of the human resource development
group who are responsible for setting up the programme will
have an important stake in the outcome of their work. They will
need to be aware of the views of trade union representatives and
will find it advisable to establish clear lines of communication by
setting up regular briefing sessions to spell out the intentions of
the development programme. Many new initiatives are made
more difficult to introduce by needlessly causing misconceptions
to arise by failing to take the opportunity to talk to people.

Vested interests

All of the people mentioned will have a vested interest in seeing that the programme meets its set objectives. By cultivating good communications, the trainer can tap into the best sources of information to check that the structure and content of the programme will be supported. This should be the time to get opinions out into the open. There is no substitute for criticism at the planning stage, because it can then be used constructively to modify the programme as necessary. Feedback has been called the 'breakfast of champions'. Without it, you are inadequately prepared for the challenges that the days bring.

Focus groups and feedback

The internal stakeholders are like an extended focus group, a think-tank that can be tapped into for guidance, reactions, insights and confirmation (or otherwise) that the development plan has the makings of success. They will be in a position to give the most effective critique of the methodology and content of the programme before and after it becomes a reality. It is therefore important to encourage communication between the programme facilitators and the stakeholders at every opportunity, and especially with the programme participants and their sponsoring managers. Ensuring constructive dialogue and criticism through-out the development programme is the aim for the trainer to achieve, even though it may not always be favourable. Without feedback, and the opportunity it gives for listening, reflecting, learning and doing something about it, the programme and all its participants – trainees and trainers – cannot hope to develop as they should.

The success of the programme will be influenced strongly by all those who are involved in implementing the strategy and designing the programme. This is why internal stakeholders are such important resources to the development team. But it is the development team of trainers who are responsible for the pro-gramme. They are the most important of all.

Small is beautiful

Only a small team of trainers is necessary to introduce a new development programme, but they must be absolutely clear about their objective and have the energy and commitment to achieve it. Ideally, they will be able to act as a self-managing team, with each member capable of initiating what needs to be done with minimal supervision. Skills will be entrepreneurial and these will probably not be evident to a great degree amongst individuals who have mainly operated in the public-service setting, but this is not a drawback if they are willing to learn them. There will be many opportunities to learn the skills needed to market and sell the proposals, to negotiate, develop business plans, manage financial resources, as well as to increase capacity in the traditional tasks of training, such as designing and delivering training sessions, ensuring the conditions are right for learning and dealing with the interpersonal interactions of groups of people.

The business of developing people

Arranging an in-house development programme is an opportunity to emphasize business development ideas and thinking amongst the development team. In the public service, there is a traditional emphasis on bureaucracy and a tendency to give what the provider thinks is needed and not what the customer needs. These attitudes have been tested in the recent past by the development of a market-led approach to public service provision. There has been greater stress on marketing. This has led to a new awareness of many traditional 'business' ideas, such as the importance of assessing the needs of clients and patients and providing cost-effective and quality responses for them.

Best-value outcomes

All outcomes of the development programme should aim at improving the ability of supervisors and other managers to ensure that their clients receive best value. It is expected that many of the lessons learned by NHS managers who have gone through the health service's recent market economics phase will be retained, as the public service sector replaces the emphasis on competition with a search for 'best value' in the way it provides for its clients.

Developing a supervisory programme gives a practical opportunity to instil good business practice into the development team. Those who run the programme will need many skills derived from the private sector. A vision of the future programme needs to be formulated and based on an awareness of the values that will be built into the programme. This leads to the definition of a strategic direction and a clear understanding of the purpose that the programme will achieve. The programme itself can then be formulated as a business plan, with all the components considered such as objectives, methods of achieving them, resources required, marketing and selling the programme, following through and evaluating the results.

The business plan for management development

Producing the business plan is a task for the total development team and the involvement of everyone in the team – including clerical and administrative support workers – should be insisted on from the outset. It is not sensible to have the plan drawn up in a vacuum by a senior team member. The result may well be workable, but it will lack the insights that the other team members can and should make. They will be expected to work the plan, and their commitment to do so will be enhanced if they have been involved in debating and defining it. The development team should approach its task in this business-like way from the beginning. By doing so the team will build a platform for effective teamworking, and as they continue to work together to implement and evaluate the programme they will provide themselves with greater opportunities to improve their performance as partners in a 'business within a business'.

Goals of human resource development

Human resource development strategies are based on the belief that people, in the main, need help to unleash much of their potential. A business that is merely surviving can get by at the level of potential currently contributed by its employees, but this will not be enough to make progress. Progress comes from the development of employees.

The goal of human resources development is the continuous improvement of the organization through its people. The supervisory development programme will be a powerful tool to extend training to employees within the organization and to provide supervisors with the ability, resources and techniques to develop themselves as better managers and to go on to develop their teams for better performance. If trainers keep this aim firmly in mind they will find that, within a short period of time, their management development strategy will produce a critical mass of supervisors who can make work-based training a practical reality by providing practical learning opportunities at the workplace.

Commitment at the top

There are other stakeholders whose involvement in successful supervisory management development is critical. The executive directorate, together with the whole of the top management, will be responsible for setting out the vision of what is to be accomplished by the programme. They need to be closely involved in the thinking that gives shape to the vision and will be influenced by discussions generated and fed by the development team.

The principle of top management commitment has been consistently promoted in the national Investors in People campaign, and it is now widely recognized that training needs to be supported by more than lip service if it is to have a real effect on the behaviour and the attitudes to organizational improvement. Commitment from the top gives credibility both to those who deliver training and to those who participate in it. The success of the supervisory programme will be directly influenced by the way it is perceived to be supported at the highest level in the organization.

Content and philosophy of development programmes

Top managers should be seen to take part in defining the content and philosophy that holds the programme together. Their under-standing of the purpose of the programme will depend on the degree to which they are made active partners in the planning process. This is the stage when senior managers will consider what they need their to-be-trained supervisors to achieve as a result of their training.

It is critical for the programme facilitator to set up lines of communication with top managers and to assist them to think through the implications of the proposed training programme. Unless there is a very frank dialogue on these lines, there will be a danger that the programme will not be based on the realistic expectations of the top management team. It would be difficult in those circumstances to produce a programme that will earn widespread respect and approval. Unless senior managers feel that they have some ownership of the programme because they have been able to mould it into shape, then sponsorship of their supervisors is not likely to be forthcoming.

Status and prestige

There is a dilemma for the trainer facilitator in all of this pre-programme consultation. Many NHS trainers feel that they lack the status in the hierarchy to take on the task of negotiating major changes in the way the organization deals with training. Supervisory training is by definition of great importance and potential value to the organization, although in much of the public service little is done to realize the potential that exists for improving the way supervisors develop. The trainer who wants to change the way supervisors and managers are developed will need a good deal of courage to seek out and enlist strong champions amongst senior managers. In this, considerations and misconceptions about relative ranking in the hierarchy have to be ignored. The trainer has a responsibility for training; by being seen to be capable of directing effective training strategies and getting results that matter to the organization, trainers will gain prestige which is worth more than status.

Involving staff representatives

Public service supervisors are likely to be members of trade unions and professional bodies, and there are sensible grounds for arranging briefing meetings with union officials to communicate the purpose of a supervisory development programme. It is useful to assess reactions to the proposal before it is launched, both within the organization and by meeting officials from the area level. Experience has proved the importance of gaining co-operation in advance of the introduction of changes in procedures.

Management may consider that the introduction of a more effective supervisory development programme is self-evidently beneficial. It has been found, however, that considerable suspicion can be aroused in organizations when a stronger emphasis is being given to management training. It is easy for the intention to be misunderstood and considered to be a way to make supervisors more effective as controllers, rather than as enablers of employee performance. Even supervisors who stand to gain from a new development programme have been less than enthusiastic, until they and their representatives have been fully briefed and have considered the implications.

This is not to suggest that training is necessarily negotiable in any formal bargaining sense, but many organizations now realize the importance of treating training as a tool to promote continuous business and personal development. It is understandable that trade unions will see the training and development field as a legitimate one for them to seek out opportunities for their members. Training and development is one area where the organization and its employees can realize the advantages of working towards the common goal of greater effectiveness. Joint consultation around the training agenda may well lead to changes in attitudes that can be the forerunners of better relationships.

Open communication leads to more open attitudes. The training strategy can be a powerful medium for building better relationships and efforts made to demonstrate good consultation will lead to long-term benefits.

Teamwork is the core value

The concept of partnership is emphasized throughout the strategy for developing supervisory management. Through partnership, it is possible to design a programme based on encouraging teamworking. Partnership demonstrates how to get the best out of working together at all stages in the programme. Different partners will be involved for their ability to contribute specific skills as the programme progresses through its development cycle. In this, the role of the development team is to learn to be a successful partnership in its own right, and then to go on from there to realize the benefits of joint working with external partners who join their network.

Many teambuilding diagnostic techniques are available to help teams identify the characteristics that combine to make an effective team. The works of Meredith Belbin and Charles Margerison, among many others, are a useful starting-point to prompt the team to begin to discover how it interacts and what it might do to improve its performance. Many other teamwork assessment instruments exist. Most are based on the analysis of questionnaires designed to measure the capacity of a team to manage the way they identify a common goal, and how well they deal with day-to-day problems by supporting each other with complementary skills in a climate of trust and openness.

The training team as exemplars of teamworking

Since the purpose of creating a management development programme is to improve the ability of managers to get the best results from themselves and their teams, it makes sense for developers to ensure that they are seen to work as an effective team. They can start by testing the diagnostic exercises on themselves.

This serves two purposes: it provides them with an insight into any blockages that affect their ability to work well together, and it will give them the necessary data from which to construct a plan to overcome the problems identified. Often, the recognition that an obstacle to effective joint working exists is sufficient to prompt team members to act differently. By practising what it will eventually teach, the development team benefits by learning more about the teambuilding process and which of the diagnostic tools on offer are best suited for use in the planned supervisory development programme.

Analysing team development needs

The decision on what type of teambuilding questionnaire to use is made on the basis of market testing. This is carried out in advance of making a final decision, by taking a random sample of supervisors who will be potential participants in the programme and getting their reactions to a selection of possible tools. Not only will this provide the development team with insights to influence their judgment but will show that they are serious in their intention to involve their clients as partners in developing the strategy.

This is basic research that will enable the development team to assess how effective supervisors are in leading their teams. Trainers should always enlist their clients in testing the diagnostic instruments and techniques that are to be used in the development programme. The information gained will give an insight into what the supervisors consider to be the most effective techniques for them. Trainers will also benefit by being able to disregard techniques that the clients are not comfortable with, and will give the development programme a greater credibility in the eyes of the customers.

Any opportunity to meet with supervisors in the preparation stage will be valuable for promoting awareness of the programme and for providing the opportunity to discuss why and how it is being set up. This will help to substitute real understanding for rumour, with useful effects on the way the programme is perceived and accepted.

Involve the customers

Involving people who stand to gain most from the successful outcome of the venture in which they have a stakeholding is a sure recipe for effective collaboration. This is the main reason for involving supervisors and senior managers within the organization. They comprise the customers and consumers of the planned training. These are two different constituencies. Customers are the fundholders – senior managers who purchase the training on behalf of their supervisors. They act as the sponsors of the supervisors. Trainers should know who holds the purse strings, for it is these managers who will need to be convinced of the case for making an investment in the new arrangements.

Financial considerations

Over recent years, public service managers have become increasingly aware of the financial reality of running their part of the organization. They expect that the human resource development function will be able to argue the business case for supervisory training, spelling out its benefits to the organization and influencing the manager to invest. In turn, fundholders must have the opportunity to talk through the intentions of the programme so they can inform the trainer of what they want the programme to achieve. There is a greater likelihood that managers will invest in the training if they are convinced that they will benefit from the improved ability of their supervisors to carry out their responsibilities with heightened understanding and competence.

It is also important to ascertain in advance how many supervisors are likely to be sponsored to the first programme, because there is an advantage to be gained by starting with a small pilot group drawn from a wide range of functions. The first intake has to be small enough to be handled properly, yet large enough to begin to make inroads into the large numbers of supervisors who will be anxious to start developing their competence.

Experience shows that there are significant benefits in having a policy to develop supervisors in multi-functional groups, especially in highly demarcated organizations like the NHS. There is a continuing need to promote integration of functions in an organization whose tribal nature leads to departmental thinking and which throws up barriers to effective teamworking as a result. By insisting on multi-functional supervisory training, the NHS trainer can provide opportunities for people from different working backgrounds to learn that they are interdependent.

Co-operation is greater than confrontation

A good supervisory training programme will soon provide evidence to support the contention that co-operation is superior to confrontation. The evidence will be seen in the heightened ability of supervisors from many different functions to work together. This is an important outcome from multi-functional training, which markedly affects future behaviour in the organization. Messages like these need not be made explicit, but they will become apparent to supervisors at a subliminal level as they reflect on the learning process that takes place in the team-learning environment.

Learning partnerships with the outside world are also valuable and any attempt to promote interaction between the in-house team of supervisors and contemporaries in other organizations will be valuable. These contacts help to encourage fresh thinking by enabling new experiences to be exchanged between different organizations.

Counteracting insularity

Trainers also have to realize that there is a danger in concentrating exclusively on their own particular training programmes. At some stage they will lose touch with developments taking place elsewhere. Their programmes will become stale and repetitious. Just as public sector organizations have found much to emulate from a study of private sector tools and techniques, so trainers can make it a part of their own continuing development to seek for innovations in the development of people, through reading books and journals, becoming actively involved in professional organizations dedicated to management development or setting up their own network of contacts with whom to keep in regular contact for the purpose of sharing best practice. The practice of benchmarking the experience of others, and setting out to adapt it to your own needs, is as advantageous to individuals as it is to organizations.

Finding tutors and mentors amongst line managers

Stakeholder discussions with fundholding managers are also important opportunities for the trainer, who needs to identify who in the organization can act as tutors or mentors in the programme. The policy of using managers to train managers has advantages and disadvantages but, on the whole, the advantages win. On the negative side is the fact that not all managers are comfortable with the role of tutor. Many fail to prepare their material and approach adequately, and this contributes to a natural lack of confidence that affects many who find themselves in front of an audience.

Many potential tutors will no doubt withdraw themselves from consideration by not volunteering to take part, but it may not always be in the best interests of the programme to accept this negative position without trying to do something about it. Experienced managers who feel like this need to be helped to find ways of sharing their experience and knowledge of the way the organization works so that supervisors can be clear about their own role as supporters of the total management effort.

Developing presentational skills

Trainers can do much to develop training and presentational skills by giving comprehensive briefing and training courses to managers who are needed to act as course tutors. Managers will value the opportunity, in sessions designed specifically to aid their personal development, to test their ability to deliver talks, lead discussion and handle the basic visual aids.

Being an effective communicator is an essential attribute of successful leaders. Efforts made to select and train managers to train others will enhance their skills and give them more confidence to communicate, not only with supervisors in the context of the development programme but also with all those whom they meet in their day-to-day affairs.

Planning, designing and delivering a training programme calls on the efforts of many people. Not all of them will be dedicated trainers, although it will be unusual if there is not a recognized trainer to co-ordinate the project and act as champion and leader of the development work.

How a development programme evolves

The training and development programme that we are describing here was the product of teamwork by a small team of trainers. It did not have the advantage of large resources of staff or training materials, because the training function had been stripped of most of its former employees in the period leading up to the reorganization to a general management structure.

When the organizational restructuring was implemented, new levels of staffing were approved for the training function and the establishment was set initially at two trainers and a part-time typist. The supervisory development programme was designed, marketed and brought to implementation through the efforts of this team, working within the levels of staffing that were affordable.

Although the size of the training resource was to increase to meet the demand for training that followed the success of the programme, there was a useful lesson for trainers to learn. It was that the training function will not get funded until it can show results. It is no use expecting to be highly resourced until you can show equally high returns on that investment. Inevitably this takes time, for learning and development have to be patiently pursued and do not happen overnight.

Better results: better funding (not the other way round)

Trainers cannot expect to be funded in advance of results, and so they tend to lose motivation. Here is where the vicious circle sets in: when trainers believe their resources are inadequate, they will often subconsciously reflect this in the level of performance they achieve. This causes the organization to maintain its current level of funding or even to reduce it. Both reactions confirm trainers in the belief that they are under-valued, and the downward spiral continues.

Many management development efforts taking place in the health and social care field are held in low esteem, even by the employers initiating them. The reasons are not hard to find. Trusts, the largest local employers of NHS staff, fail to realize that training is an investment in the future, and that investment in the development of managers ought to be a high priority. That it is not may be judged by the relatively small number of employing organizations in the public service that have achieved the national Investors in People standard. Training budgets are always under pressure, as are all budgets that cannot be readily seen to contribute to direct patient care, but the total amount spent in the NHS on training of all types is very considerable. The problem is in the distribution of resources into management development.

Invest in success

It is far better if trainers adopt a success strategy from the beginning and work to get the best out of the resources they have. Actions speak louder than words, and evidence that good work is being done will gain a greater reward in the long run.

Trainers need to design some way of measuring the contribution that training makes in financial terms if they are to convince the fundholders that they are worth more. We will return to this issue in the chapter dealing with the evaluation of the benefits of training.

CHAPTER 5

Design

Structured development

The development of the programme follows a basic and simple formula to provide a structure for the process. Brian Tracy, a pre-eminent educator in the field of personal development, has called this the GOSPA formula. The acronym stands for Goals, Objectives, Strategies, Plans and Actions. Work in each of these stages gives strategic direction to people involved in a project and enables them to carry out the steps in a logical sequence. This ensures that initial inertia is transformed into momentum that keeps all involved in the activity on track.

Our goal is to build supervisors who can transform their teams into the kind of performers that they are destined to be. The vision is to provide a development programme that will give supervisors the support they need to change their behaviour into transformational leadership, a term that best describes the role which modern supervisors are increasingly being required to carry out.

Many supervisors who were interviewed when the development programme was being planned said that they did not consistently produce results that succeeded in getting the best either from themselves or from their teams. This was not because they felt they lacked the innate ability and personal resources to do so, but because they considered that selection and training for their role was inadequate. The hypothesis we set out to prove was that better training would change this perception, and that supervisors would respond to the support given through the programme and become better at achieving the results that mattered.

The NHS and the public service in general are not alone in recruiting supervisors from the ranks and expecting them to be able to carry out a demanding role with the minimum of training. Experience in the job has, after all, been considered to be the way managers have traditionally been developed. This is an inadequate and unproductive system for dealing with management succession, and its ideas should be challenged in any development strategy for supervisors.

A phased programme for development

Phase 1 The first five days

The development programme was designed to be carried out in three phases. The first phase, lasting a week, dealt with supervision in the context of the organization. This introductory section was split into two parts. The first, lasting two days, took the form of a conventional series of talks covering the mission and values of the organization, its structure, and the objectives and challenges facing it. The next three days were devoted to in-depth presentations, role-plays and case studies on the responsibilities and role of the supervisor in meeting organizational objectives. Each talk was interspersed with participative group discussions, which had the dual purposes of promoting individual participation and reinforcing the learning process.

Phase 2 The second five days

The second five-day phase concentrated on five separate modules dealing with specific management skills. These topics emerged from discussions with managers and supervisors during the market research consultations, and were incorporated into the proposed training programme at the planning stage. The topics that supervisors believed to be important to them were:

- action-centred leadership
- communications

- information technology
- human relations
- effective presentation

These topics were presented in separate modular workshops, each lasting one day. All were highly participative and were designed to highlight and enhance skills that would be required in the final phase of the programme – that in which supervisors worked together in teams to solve operational problems.

Phase 3 The last eight days

The third and final phase consisted of a series of one-day sessions devoted to project work, undertaken by teams formed of programme participants. The supervisors were released over a period of eight Fridays. They were assigned a real-life issue that had been selected by their top management, and were required to research the issue, consider how it might be resolved, and produce a comprehensive proposal that would deal with the problem. This project-work phase builds on the knowledge, skills and insights which have been learned on the programme.

The programme concludes with each team presenting the project report containing proposals for action to an audience of the senior managers who commissioned the work, together with their peers and colleagues. The project action-learning phase is without doubt the most valuable learning experience in the programme and will be considered in more detail later.

Adding value through applied learning

It is essential to incorporate an applied learning stage to demonstrate how the learning gained in the training programme can be translated into practical effect. Unless the knowledge and skills acquired in the programme can be translated into action and get results, effective learning does not happen, and the whole process will fail. By integrating theory with practice in this action-based learning programme, we gained valuable evidence that the process achieved exceptional results in terms of personal and organizational development.

Personal development is recognizable in the way supervisors respond to the challenge of the project. Not only does each team have to draw on their own resources to beat the intense time pressure they are under. They also know that their senior managers expect them to present the most effective solution to their assigned problem when all the teams take part in the end-of-programme project presentations. The competitive factor clearly plays an important part in giving additional drive to team efforts.

The organization also gains because many of the recommended new practices that are proposed by the teams will be implemented subsequently. These results are a complete vindication of the contention that effective training can lead to improved performance. Moreover, many of the solutions are so effective in overcoming long-standing problems that the added value gained from the new procedures far outweighs the financial cost of putting the supervisors through the programme.

Introduction to learning

The theoretical part of the course was conceived as being an introduction to the learning process for people who had possibly not experienced such a concentrated learning event before. We needed to make the event user-friendly, in the sense that the learning atmosphere would be supportive, there would be a minimum of 'rules', and the purpose of every part of the process would be explained in advance so that people would know why it was included, as well as how it would be useful. The intention was to create a climate conducive to real learning from the beginning. Following are some of the ways we achieved this.

Training venues

The theoretical part of the programme held in the first two weeks is conducted in a classroom location. This does not have to be purpose built, though it is obviously preferable if a separate training centre is available. If it is not, there are many venues that can be adapted to serve as training centres in most health care organizations. Trainers are by nature contrivers, and it is not difficult to find ways of setting up a central base for learning.

Where the catchment area for course members is spread over a large geographical area, there is the possibility of setting up satellite training centres. These would complement the corporate training strategy, and could also be the centre for adding specific training as required by that locality.

Certain minimum requirements have to be assured if course members are to feel reasonably comfortable. Chief amongst these is good lighting, especially in the presentation area where visual displays, such as overhead and slide projectors, video recorders and flip charts need to be visible from all parts of the room. This may be stating the obvious, but it is not unusual for trainers to be delivering overhead projections in a room where the ambient lighting from windows is so strong that it cancels out the picture on the screen.

If it can be contrived, try to have a raised stage built in at the end of the room where presentations are made. This will have a major effect on the quality of the presentations by giving them greater visibility, as well as adding a psychological impact to the proceedings. This setting will be especially powerful for staging end-of-programme team presentations to large audiences, as when the action learning teams of supervisors present their problem-solving project reports.

Warmth is also important. Classroom learning is a sedentary occupation for the course members, a fact often not appreciated by a trainer who is fired up with enthusiasm and adrenalin and able to move about. As body temperature decreases so attention falls off, and this adds an unnecessary restriction on people's ability to concentrate on learning.

Care should be taken to inject some active learning events into the programme, if possible into each session in the day. This is easily managed by arranging short (say, five-minute) recapitula-tion summaries at the end of a lecture session, on the following lines.

The time allowance for a lecture topic should be about 45 minutes; any longer and effectiveness will suffer from the law of diminishing returns. The final five minutes of the session can be spent productively on what might be called 'active reflection'.

Recording learning

Active reflection is the process of giving each course member the time and space to mentally review the lecture and identify the key points from it that are felt to be important. These points are written into their personal learning portfolio, which is a course journal or logbook. The main purpose of the portfolio is to provide the learner with a convenient way of capturing the essential information given in the course.

This exercise achieves a number of useful learning goals. The act of reflecting on an event is a fundamental part of the process of learning for everyone. By reserving a period of time for reflection throughout the programme, we are reminding people of this essential, but generally under-used, activity.

The active reflection period helps to focus thinking back onto the main points of the topic that has been presented, and so gives an opportunity for the course members to recall the messages that are relevant and important to them.

Writing these points in the learning portfolio provides a record that can be referred to from time to time in the future, so helping to reinforce learning and memory.

Successful group discussions

There is a further stage to active reflection that turns it from being initially a solitary study into a useful group exercise. This next stage is done at the end of the day, when the last fifteen-minute period is set aside for consolidating the results of each of the preceding individual reflection periods into one final round of group discussion.

The group discussion works like this. The total group is subdivided into sets of two or three people. They are asked to conduct a joint review of the points that each of them has recorded during the day and summarize them into a list, in priority order of perceived importance. The list is printed in bullet-point format and displayed so that it can be easily read by the full group.

The sheets of key learning points are then displayed for the total group to discuss. The group gains from being able to scan the points that have been considered to be of value, and they can debate the relative weighting that has been given to the points by the different subgroups. This further consolidates the day's learning.

It is common to find that these final recapitulation sessions raise interesting questions about the content and delivery of the lecture sessions. This will give trainers useful guidance in identifying what needs to be improved in subsequent sessions.

There is another benefit to the process. This is an exercise that calls for high levels of interpersonal skills. It will be found that this exercise, if practised regularly, will also help people to develop their soft skills, such as listening skills, negotiating skills, and the ability to set priorities.

The learning portfolio

Reference has been made to the learning portfolio, which is a personal record of progress through the programme kept by each participant. The portfolio is a significant feature in the learning toolbox and its importance needs to be clearly understood by each course member. Trainers therefore have a duty to explain the significance and use of the portfolio at the pre-course briefing when the programme is outlined.

The portfolio is an important aid to learning because it provides learners with a record of their involvement in the learning programme. The portfolio record will also be assessed by the course assessor at the end of the programme, so that progress through the course can be judged.

The portfolio is issued to course members in the form of a substantial A4 lever-arch file having a 2½ inch paper capacity. At the outset it contains only the course programme, syllabus, timetable and list of participants. If desired, it may be colour-coded to differentiate the members of the action-learning groups into which the total course membership is divided. The label area is completed by the owner with name, job title, place of work, and the name and dates of the development programme.

This is the empty shell into which the course member will deposit the lecture notes, handouts and other materials used to support the various training sessions attended. Individuals will add their own commentaries on the various learning events, their active learning reflections, details of case studies and other exercises used in the programme, and anything they consider is relevant or useful, and which adds a new dimension to their learning experience. This impels people to think more widely around the issues examined in their programme, and can provide an outlet for considerable creativity in the exercise of discovery learning.

The portfolio is a compendium of learning. It will be used as a reference manual, and many supervisors who have compiled a portfolio to support their learning have spoken of its value as a memory jogger in later years. The portfolio is a useful source of inspiration when faced with workplace difficulties – many of the techniques and practices that are contained in it can be used to deal with problems that arise in the future.

All portfolios are individual and will reflect the individuality of the compiler in the range and richness of the information which is filed. There is no set list of what should or should not be included, but most compilers will ensure that their contents are clearly categorized and filed into separate sections for easy reference. A contents list showing these broad categories will be a help to the assessor.

Accreditation for management development

We have seen that it was important to have the organization's management development programmes accredited by an external accrediting body. Eventually, all the three separate levels of management development were accredited by the Institute for Supervision and Management, in addition to the internal assessment arrangements conducted by the organization itself. The portfolio is an essential part of these assessment processes.

Planning for results

One of the elements of assessment in the supervisory development programme is the review of the action plans that candidates incorporate into their portfolios in order to identify the work they will do to transfer their course learning into a practical work-based project. Candidates are required to give details of the outcomes they achieve in carrying out these projects, and give clear commentaries on the benefits resulting from their innovation. Here, the assessor is looking for proof that the essential lessons have been learned and that, as a result, the supervisor has planned how that learning can lead to needed changes in the workplace.

It can be argued that writing an action plan to build on the knowledge gained in a tutorial is by no means the same as putting it into effect. This would be accepted as a justified criticism, were it not for the fact that there is a safeguard to ensure that actions are put into practice.

The safeguard is that the in-house trainer, together with the manager who sponsored the supervisor, are committed to following up the progress of action plans. Moreover, the course members know this.

Following up the action plans

There are certain logistical reasons that do not make it possible to follow up every action plan made by every supervisor. There would be too many plans, and too little time available to cover them all. However, the system that works well is to follow up on a random basis by collecting information on progress over a six-month period after the end of the programme. It is then possible to compile some statistical evidence about the outcomes that are achieved by supervisors.

The portfolios of participants are discussed in the end-of-programme debriefings that take place between the supervisor and the sponsoring manager. These sessions are mandatory and are principally for the supervisor to present a written and oral critique of the programme to the sponsor.

The course critique

Another quality-control measure is the course critique, which supervisors are required to produce at the end of the programme. Course critiques have been introduced to provide information to the manager and to the trainer about the supervisor's perception of the programme. This is a considered opinion which has to be written up and put into a structured form. Views are asked for on three topics:

- Did the programme meet the objectives you set?
- In what ways are you now able to perform more effectively as a supervisor?
- Describe a project that you could now manage that will improve your section.

Promoting continuity of learning

The last topic has been found especially productive in generating effective action to deal with often long-standing problem areas. The reason we believe it to be important is that the answer makes the manager aware that the programme has been able to unlock confidence and ability in the supervisor. The ensuing discussion of the kind of project the supervisor would like to undertake becomes goal-centred around practical achievements which the manager and supervisor can agree are needed. In focusing on changes to make the working situation more productive, the manager has a golden opportunity to offer support to the supervisor by allowing the project to go ahead. There are excellent results to be gained from this approach, and managers who give these projects the green light find that their confidence in the supervisor is amply rewarded.

The portfolio as feedback mechanism

The feedback from managers who have taken part in debriefing meetings has consistently referred to the usefulness of the portfolio as a talking-point. It is almost as though the portfolio is a road map of the journey to personal development that the supervisor has taken. It allows both manager and supervisor to explore the development programme and trace how it has linked the various training needs together and met them with a logical and all-embracing learning process.

Sponsoring managers are also impressed at the range and depth of learning that is absorbed during the programme. This in turn has been known to lead the manager to take up further management development opportunities. It was the emergence of such a need that enabled the training function to extend the initial supervisory development programme that is featured here, by adding an introductory programme for aspiring supervisors and a higher diploma level programme for middle and senior managers.

Planning for promotion

Supervisors are often selected for promotion because they have performed well as teamworkers in their previous jobs, but it is not always wise to predict future performance on the basis of past performance in a completely different job. Many of the characteristics of the effective worker will be carried over into the new role because they are an inherent part of the basic make-up of the individual. Personal attributes such as the ability to get on with others, being keen and willing, displaying aptitude and talent, motivation and attitude, are all selection components that need to be resolved when making a decision to promote. But today's supervisor needs the ability to rapidly assimilate and become effective in a variety of different skills that have never been called into play before.

Consequently, the transition to supervisor calls for planned development to identify what makes for effective management in the context of the particular organization at that specific time, and then help can be designed in a tailor-made programme to develop the attributes that will be needed.

Researching programme content from organizational reports

The market research conducted with senior managers during the earlier planning stage provides many pointers to what needs to be incorporated into the programme. There are some additional sources of information that can throw light on issues that will affect the organization in the future, and which will consequently need to be dealt with by managers. Business plans produced by units of management, such as Trusts, directorates and departments, are a prime source of study when considering the objectives that are to be achieved in the next planning cycle. These objectives should be analysed and the management skills required to reach those objectives identified. By comparing these against the skills presently available, the trainer will know where training effort should be directed. This approach ensures that the development programme concentrates on specific skills, and in this way the training is focused on the organization's primary needs.

How competent are supervisors now?

Organizational objectives are attained through the efforts of people, and the way in which human and other resources are deployed in the organization is the concern of management and, at the operational level, of supervisory management. Trainers designing a development programme are required to assess, in discussion with line managers, whether supervisors possess the skills and knowledge needed to give them the best chance to attain the objectives. Supervisors have to answer the question, 'Do you have the depth and range of competences that are necessary to ensure that these objectives will be attained?' and their managers have to be involved in making good any shortfall. The answers will determine the blueprint for designing a management development programme to target both the needs of the individual and those of the organization.

This enquiry has to be conducted with tact, often on a one-to-one basis at first, until a degree of trust has been created to allow for frank discussion of what are essentially individual weaknesses. The topics that individuals identify as training and development needs will be diverse, and each supervisor will have a personal repertoire of skills that require up-dating. By recording and analysing these it is possible to define the needs that are most commonly distributed amongst supervisors. This brings out the core categories which require attention, and provides the building blocks for the development programme.

The five key barriers approach

It has been found that a relatively simple telephone questionnaire, based on asking supervisors to name the five most difficult aspects of their job, has given all the information from which to produce a cross-section of training needs just as relevant as that discovered in more costly, time-consuming and extensive research.

In practice, this analysis is relatively simple, and its simplicity leads some critics to say it lacks academic and statistical rigour. In its favour is the fact that this identification of training needs does home in on the common denominators of need that are shared widely through the supervisory management population, independent of the sector or industry in which they work. This is a useful way of bypassing the seemingly interminable analyses that can bog trainers down for months before they feel prepared to begin the training that their clients are expecting.

Interpersonal qualities and the development of soft skills

Since their management role is predominantly concerned with managing people, supervisors very frequently feel the need to improve their interpersonal capabilities if they are to get the best out of their teams. They will want to be better in the areas of the so-called 'soft' skills. So such broad topics as communication, leadership, teamworking and teambuilding, dealing with people, setting goals and standards, motivating and delegating, will be found high on the list.

A recent national survey of 1500 members of the human resources professions, of whom a quarter were in the public sector, indicated that the top five soft skills seen as being most important for new entrants from college were oral communication, teamworking, listening, written communication and problem-solving. The overwhelming majority of respondents recognized the implications of these soft skills for their organization.

Given this information it must make sense to ensure that these skills are developed by people in the organization, not only for new entrants but also for existing staff. It will be seen that these are the skills that are going to be needed by supervisors during the problem-solving stage of their programme.

A development programme should aim to improve the way supervisors use soft skills in dealing with their own people. In time, greater awareness of the importance of developing good interpersonal relationships may encourage a change away from traditional closed and repressive attitudes to more participative and open styles of managing.

In addition, a supervisory programme should develop other abilities that the supervisor needs for success. Foremost is the need for supervisors to exercise strategic thinking in dealing with the changes that continually face them. Being able to manage implies that the ramifications of change can be foreseen and options for dealing with them can be planned before a course of action is decided.

Pro-action versus reaction

Many problems of supervision stem from the essentially reactive nature of managing at the front line. Because change is not thought through, supervisors fail to plan for contingencies until they are hit with the effects of change. Fire-fighting then becomes the norm and fire prevention, which requires strategic thinking, is again put off to another day that never comes. An effective development programme will design ways of promoting innovation and creativity into the learning structure to emphasize the role of the leader as a strategic thinker.

An important way of developing a strategic thinking capacity in supervisors is to require them, as a part of their job, to engage their teamworkers in joint problem-solving using a range of creative thinking techniques. This approach mirrors the problem-solving part of their own training programme. They know that the system works, because they have seen the results that can be achieved. By using a problem-solving approach with their teams, supervisors will improve their effectiveness as managers, and bring about changes that will motivate their people and give them more job satisfaction.

Clarifying the supervisory context – induction and orientation

Another component of the development programme will deal with the context in which the supervisor operates. All employees are more effective when they know what they are setting out to accomplish. This knowledge is essential if they are to contribute their special talents fully to the enterprise. This is the purpose of induction and orientation training, the process of providing new employees with a road map that points out the landmarks and makes them familiar with organizational aims and practices.

Induction is also essential to provide some sort of orientation to the supervisor, who is entering into a new job and a different world and needs help in finding a way around the new experience. That is why some part of the introductory phase of the development programme is spent in activities that help to place the supervisor into the organizational context. This will provide a global view, enabling them to see how the organization has been shaped by the changes through which it has gone. All organizations are constantly undergoing structural change and the changes that have acted on the NHS during its 50 years of existence have been inexorable, intense and unremitting. This change is continuing at an increasing pace, with the consequence that NHS employees – and managers in particular – experience high levels of stress in their daily working lives.

The reality of the NHS is that it exists to satisfy the human need to have health and have it more abundantly. This purpose makes the pursuit of change in the NHS inevitable, leading it to seek continually for new and better and more costly treatments and technologies to satisfy an insatiable demand. The NHS is faced with an ultimately impossible task. The inevitability of change, and the paradox that the main objective of the NHS is never likely to be reached, forms the reality in which managers develop. The introduction of the supervisor into this reality should be addressed in the orientation phase of their development, in a way that tries to counter that negative picture with a more optimistic one.

Encouraging positive attitudes

The training process is more likely to be rewarding and get memorable results if it is conducted in a spirit of optimism and enthusiasm. These are positive attitudes to be encouraged in the programme. Through training and development the organization can help and support people to become the achievers that they are meant to be, and can encourage them to explore the opportunities that exist for making better futures for themselves and for the organization of which they are a part. The development of supervisors should be a period in which they can reflect on how to achieve lasting benefits in the workplace and plan new ways of dealing with the problems of the day. The benefits of their development will be seen when they apply these ideas on return to their jobs.

CHAPTER 6

Marketing

The management developer needs to be skilful in marketing and selling the supervisory development programme. Launching new products into any marketplace calls for the use of marketing techniques and selling skills to find out what the customer needs, so that the products or services which are delivered will be the ones the customer can be induced to buy. Many public service departments still fail to understand the importance of marketing their services. They do not recognize that the market in which they work is customer-driven and no different in principle from any other market that exists to satisfy the purchaser. This lack of perception is gradually changing throughout the public services but there are still many examples showing that it is what the provider wishes to give that over-rides what the customer needs to receive.

Marketing is critical

Trainers, whether in the public or private sector, often do not fully understand the crucial importance that marketing plays in the running of a business. They may fail to appreciate that the human resource development function is a business within a business. The business of the human resource development function is to support the need of the whole organization to operate at optimum capacity, and trainers have to consider how the contribution they make will enable people to meet organizational goals.

The trainer as entrepreneur

Trainers, especially those in the public sector, who actively set out to market their services within the organization gradually learn to develop a different mind-set. They foster a more entrepreneurial outlook that enables them to connect more closely with the ultimate business goals of their organization. This will encourage a different way of looking at the service they provide. Encouraging an entrepreneurial paradigm leads the trainer to search for opportunities to act creatively, not rigidly, and to take calculated risks rather than maintain the status quo. The decision to learn more about marketing, and to apply the lessons learned to change the way the supervisory programme is set up, is a step towards self-development for the trainer.

Establishing a training programme is as much a learning opportunity for trainers as it is for participants. A trainer who takes on the challenge of creating better management development embarks on a voyage of self-discovery through continuing personal and professional development.

If human resource developers are the marketers, then the managers buying into management development are their customers. As such, they are entitled to expect the best support they can get to help them perform effectively, and trainers should be constantly seeking creative ways to meet this need. This is the marketing message for trainers and is the key to their producing innovative and satisfying management programmes.

Selling the dream of lifelong learning

Marketing management development calls for a kind of evangelical zeal that stems from the conviction that organizations can only grow if the right conditions for developing their employees are in place. The trend towards lifelong learning recognizes that human potential is under-used. People are unable or unwilling to take up many of the learning opportunities that are all around them, and they need help to do so.

Organizations can play an important part in supporting lifelong learning by recognizing that their employees have aspirations for self-actualization, and helping them to do something positive about it. Increasingly, human resource development functions are encouraging innovative training programmes to provide for the mutual advantage of employees and the organization.

The acquisition of knowledge in itself is not enough, however. A learner requires more than the ability to increase the capacity to know about things. Sufficient time and space needs to be given for reflecting on experience, to think through the lessons learned, and to find ways of applying those lessons to improve future situations. Learning takes time, and often organizations do not take a long-term view of the investment they make into training. They expect immediate results, and fail to recognize that lifelong learning is by definition a long-term investment in the continuous improvement of people.

Human resource professionals who are aware of this correlation between training investment and organizational improvement have to ensure that the message is understood at the top of the organization if they are to improve their influence and attract financial resources to training and development.

Any programme for management development is a Trojan horse in a strategy to enhance organizational performance. The influential trainer recognizes that actions count for more than words and will concentrate on designing a development programme that is based on the broad concept of continuous improvement.

Supervisors as trainers

By aiming the development programme at supervisors, the trainer will target a section of management that has the greatest opportunity to influence and extend the principles of lifelong learning amongst the workforce itself. Supervisors who have experienced the benefits of good training can learn how to train others. By demonstrating the effect that the development programme has had on their own performance, supervisors by their own example can lead others to see the advantages of practising continuous personal development for themselves. Creating a cohort of leader/trainers at the operational level allows the organization to build up an invaluable resource to change the future.

Training is about changing behaviour

The rationale for training and development needs to be promoted consistently and carefully. One purpose of training is to help people to behave differently, to act in ways that encourage them to achieve goals more efficiently. The wider purpose is to instil a philosophy and practice of achievement into the organization so that its employees are motivated to excel and are provided with the means of doing so.

These purposes combine to promote a climate receptive to new thinking and form the basis for the management development programme. They describe the vision for the programme. The effort to transform this vision into reality is directed mainly into the design and delivery of the training. But first, attention has to focus on selling the dream.

The trainer setting out to introduce a new supervisory development programme will soon realize whether or not the organization is receptive to new thinking, particularly where the acceptance of new training arrangements is concerned. Introducing training needs to be handled with diplomacy and firmness, bearing in mind the often-quoted observation of Machiavelli, who wrote:

> There is nothing more difficult to plan, more doubtful of success, nor more dangerous to manage than the creation of a new system. For the initiator has the enmity of all who would profit by the preservation of the old institutions, and merely lukewarm defenders in those who should gain by the new ones.

Combatting the enemies of change

A strategy to improve how supervisors are developed is an exercise in influencing the way the organization thinks and in changing that paradigm. Substituting new creativity for old routines has to begin by shifting mind-sets. Good marketing will aim to move attitudes away from the familiar routines and open up the prospect of changing the way they are carried out. Training and development can be a subtle means of promoting more flexible thinking and should be used as a tool for change-making.

The effect of the development programme will be measured by its ability to give supervisors the knowledge and skills they need to carry out their role competently. However, more subtle effects will be found in the way the programme can change attitudes and behaviours, and an example of this is found in the effect the action-learning phase has on promoting self-sufficiency in supervisors. This project work is particularly important in imparting the need to cope out of their own resources with problems.

Development projects

One of the outcomes of the development programme is to give supervisors the opportunity to use their initiative and resourcefulness. Morris and Burgoyne, in their book *Developing Resourceful Managers*, were suggesting as long ago as the 1970s that resourceful managers were a vital need in Britain.

They advocated that development projects, combining individual career advantage and organizational interests, should be a primary means of enabling managers to develop themselves, and that management development as a function needed to be reinvigorated to tackle this need. Two decades later, these common-sense suggestions have generally failed to be implemented into management development programmes at the local, grass-roots operational level, yet it is there that they are likely to show their most powerful effects on people.

In-house development programmes for supervisors and managers should aim to give their participants every opportunity to employ the self-reliance that they are often unable to exercise fully in their organizational role. Large bureaucracies in particular impose subtle restrictions on the capacity of their employees to act on their own initiative. It is often the training programme that provides the right kind of environment for encouraging self-reliant behaviour. The expectation is that once supervisors have experienced this quality as a feature of their personal development, they will feel the need to make it a characteristic of their working life.

Training and development specialists have a responsibility to incorporate activities into their training strategies that encourage and reward the resourcefulness of participants, if they are to help supervisors to meet present day challenges with imagination and resolve.

CHAPTER 7

Communication

Scratch deep enough beneath the surface of a problem and you get to people – and communication. Anyone who works through the stages leading to a fully fledged supervisory development programme will be following a badly signposted road into uncharted territory. Messages to and from all concerned in the development will be garbled. There will be ample opportunity to reflect on the truth of the maxim, 'the meaning of your communication is the response you get', on any number of occasions when the message you gave is demonstrably not the message that someone received, was wrongly acted on, and so caused another problem which had to be rectified.

Communication and leadership

A new supervisory development programme needs leadership and leadership needs to use communication as an essential tool for change-making. The first of many issues that the change-maker has to resolve is how to create a good communication system that supports the programme and enables it to work effectively, at all stages from inception to the evaluation of its results.

Getting communications right is a prime responsibility of the trainer who is designing the programme. Trainers show they are putting communication effectiveness at the top of their priority list by setting up an efficient consultation process. This has to provide an example to others, and should be a clear demonstration of how to plan and present messages between people in the organization.

The need to be better communicators will assuredly be a high priority for supervisors who take part in the development pro-gramme. It is essential that they can rely on the quality of the communication which is given by trainers if they are to be confident in the training they will be given in this essential skill.

Better communication – a universal need

The need to improve personal communication, or some variant of this, will without doubt be found in the list of training needs generated in the pre-course market research. If it is missing, then either the inquiry methodology was wrong, or people are delud-ing themselves. Communication is one of the most important keys to effective management, and ensuring that supervisors are profi-cient communicators is a key component of the training they need to undertake. Careful consideration has to be given to the enhancing of this skill.

Communication is seen as well as heard, and the way the organization sends its messages can sometimes be confusing. Something is wrong when the messages given out are not sup-ported by accompanying actions. A case in point is often found in policy statements that speak of people being the organization's greatest asset, and profess the intention to train and develop them. This will sound hollow if little is done to provide the training that is promised.

Conversely, an organization which embarks on a sound strategy to train and develop, and concentrates its efforts initially on the supervisory level of management, will gain credibility for the integrity of its communication.

Communicating commitment

Supervisory development needs to be seen to have the support of the chief executive. Lip service is not sufficient. The most success-ful training programmes are found where the chief executive is seen to endorse the process from the beginning. Programme participants are quick to recognize whether top management is committed to their development, and no amount of well-intentioned platitudes can substitute for their recognition that top management is actively overseeing the training strategy to make sure that it works.

Actions that count in the eyes of programme participants are simple and need not be time-consuming. A start can be made by having the chief executive write a personal letter to congratulate each delegate on being selected for the programme. The letter should point out the importance of personal and organizational development, and state that the end of the programme will be marked with a special session at which the chief executive and other top directors will meet the supervisors and review their progress.

This advance notice of intention allows top management to set aside time in their diaries well in advance of the planned meeting, and gives supervisors the message that top managers really support the programme. This simple communication has been found to have an extraordinary effect on the morale and commitment of programme participants.

Linking the partners; selling the service

The trainer is the key to setting up effective communications between all the partners in the development programme. Trainers should take the responsibility for establishing the linkages that bind partners together and in particular for influencing their chief executive to act as a visible supporter of development in the organization.

How can trainers go about enhancing their strategic role and bring the case for better training before the decision-makers? Many trainers say that they want to give training and development a higher profile, enhance its strategic focus, and ensure it is recognized as a force for changing organizational performance for the better. Why then is it frequently found that this desirable outcome is not achieved?

The reality often is that trainers believe that they are not able to argue their corner in the higher echelons of the organization, either because they doubt their own ability or because they are constrained by a bureaucratic, status-conscious and hierarchical system that can frustrate their best intentions to open up lines of communication. This is especially so in public services, where many trainers still have a long way to go to get their role and services acknowledged as being important.

Part of the reason for this is that trainers do not sell their services. Many remain suspicious of the marketing concept and believe it to be a commercial practice that is in some way at odds with the ethos of public service. This attitude has slowly changed as business practices and business thinking have become better understood and have been more entrenched in the running of public services, but many trainers still have to learn that marketing is the essential route to success in business, and the business of training has to be marketed just like any other.

Proposal for development

A first step is to put together a discussion paper to position the development programme as the preferred management tool to improve competitiveness. Trainers should open the debate on a wide front, get reactions and comments, and take time to compile a report that will provide a strategic direction for debate.

This paper will be an essential first step in the process of clarifying thinking, looking at the options, and producing a considered hypothesis on which to build the case for a development programme. The widest consensus of views should be sought from all those who have a contribution to make in shaping the paper. If significant decision-makers can readily discern the presence of their own views in the paper, the more likely they will be to support it when it is submitted for acceptance as a policy document.

The purpose of the proposal is to set out the reasons for the development programme, the methodology to be used in implementing it, costs to be incurred, and the benefits that will be achieved. Aim for a simple format, keep it short, put the executive summary onto one page, and make certain it contains all the key factors that will be needed to clearly define the case and enable a decision to be made to implement it.

Presentation

Presentation is always important, so make the proposal look important by binding it professionally. There can be no excuses for spelling mistakes, typographical errors and the like, but do not rely on the spellcheck facility on word processors. Remember the telling words familiar to many typists:

> I has a spelling checker
> It comes with my PC.
> It plainly marks for my revue
> Mistake I cannot sea.
> I've ran this poem threw it,
> I'm sure your please to no.
> Its letter perfect in its weigh
> My checker tolled me so.

Proofreading

Learn to proofread – there are some essential techniques for training yourself to home in on mistakes. Do it thoroughly before sending out the paper to a selected cross-section of readers who can be relied on to comment constructively on the content. Prepare a final version from this consultation and arrange to present the paper to the management team. The chances of reaching a decision to proceed with the development programme are significantly improved by planning the approach in this way, and the prospects of successful implementation are enhanced by having the seal of approval of top management on the initiative.

This is not to suggest though that a development programme needs express permission to be granted before it can be introduced. The trainer in an organization has the responsibility to train as part of the employment contract. It is, however, more effective to approach the introduction of a new development programme from a business-like perspective and take all steps necessary to present it in the context of organizational strategy, if only to give it the importance that it deserves.

A programme which is planned to make a significant impact on the way the organization develops its managers has to be scrutinized by top management. This is an example of using communication to enhance the profile of the trainer and the development function as well as that of the supervisors at whom the programme is targeted.

Communicating the intent

Supporting the development programme with a planned communications strategy calls for continuous action. The fact that the programme can go ahead has to be made known throughout the organization, especially in those departments from which potential programme participants will be selected. The traditional and necessary medium for communicating with heads of department is by sending memoranda, and this will be done, but it is not sufficient.

It is far better to set up briefing sessions first. Invite heads of department, together with their senior managers, to a presentation that covers all the key issues which have gone into the proposal that went to the executive directors. Take them step by step through the why and the how of supervisory development as you aim to practise it in the organization. The aim is more than to impart knowledge about the programme – it is to promote understanding by giving the opportunity to have questions asked and answered. This will go far to create the right conditions for having the ideas accepted with enthusiasm. Remember Machiavelli, and try to defuse the opposition that is always under the surface when innovation is in the air.

Minimizing the threat of change by discussion

Innovators need to take every opportunity to make potential change less threatening to those who will be affected by it, and a full discussion of the process before it is thrust upon an unsuspecting world may be the best way to deal with fear of the unknown. Once the face-to-face presentations have been concluded, follow-up memoranda can be issued to record the proceedings and act as reinforcement to the message.

Allocating responsibility

A part of the message that needs to be spelled out is that heads of departments will be primarily responsible for identifying those of their supervisors who should be put forward for training. It follows that department heads will need to be clear on the criteria for selection laid down for the development programme. To ensure that the criteria are understood and applied equitably may require the trainer to offer to support selectors through the selection process. If enquiries show there is a need for this, a longer time-scale may have to be allowed for preselection training.

Involving participants in the change process

The next link in the communication chain is to the supervisors. Every supervisor, without exception, should have an internal mailing about the opportunity for professional development being introduced. Every supervisor is entitled to know that their future development is to be addressed, even though it will not be possible for all of them to be part of the launch programme. Full disclosure shows that the organization is serious about developing its supervisors for career progression. It also enables the trainer to open up a direct line of communication with prospective clients and to compile a database listing all the supervisors in the organization at first hand. The size of this list will certainly show the magnitude of the task ahead.

The newsletter

It is essential to keep closely connected to supervisory managers, and a decision needs to be made on the feasibility of establishing a regular training newsletter. The first edition of this could be a simple one-sheet publication, issued when the first wave of candidates for the inaugural course are being selected. It would contain details about the aims and objectives of the development programme, its date, time and venue, the criteria for selection, and how to apply for a place, with a tear-off portion to be completed with personal details and returned to a central clearing-point for further information to be issued.

The idea of a training newsletter provides a useful way for trainers to bridge the communications gap and sell their service. There will be a time-cost in compiling the publication, but this will be offset by the value of promoting the organization's commitment to training and advertising the benefits of training that is on offer to managers and employees. The newsletter is an important measure that should be taken to drive home the message that training has a positive role in the organization.

Listening to the voices of customers

The communication system also has to provide opportunities for the trainer to listen to the voices of the customers. This means establishing formal and informal channels to supervisors on the programme, and to their managers. The supervisors' reactions and comments are relatively easy to obtain, through formal questionnaire surveys or by informal discussion. Both of these methods are prompted by the trainer and can be used with senior managers, but it will be useful to arrange for the sponsoring manager and the supervisor who is nominated to the programme to talk through the programme together and share their personal perceptions of its value as a medium for development. This critique provides the sponsoring managers with valuable insights into the supervisors' reactions to the programme and enables them to discuss how this newfound knowledge, and the skills and attitudes gained on the programme, can be used in the workplace.

Recording communications to stimulate learning

Communication can be an ephemeral pursuit. Messages are rapidly generated but just as quickly lost. Deciding what to record, and having the discipline to reflect on the record, is a sure way to gain advantage from the wealth of information that is developed in the supervisory programme.

This information needs to be captured, for it is the key to learning how to improve the programme so that it can be continuously fine-tuned to meet the changing needs expressed by the participants. Only by keeping in touch with the customers' needs, by talking and listening to them, can providers find out whether their efforts are giving the expected results.

This is why the successful trainer will build a network of communicating systems around the supervisory development programme and will ensure that regular set periods are set aside to learn from the information collected.

CHAPTER 8

Implementation

The preparation that has gone into the programme, in discussing the initial idea of transforming supervisory management development, doing the market research, and enlisting support to introduce a prototype programme will have slowly formed a mental picture of how the programme will be implemented. We have described how ideas gain credibility and a sense of purpose through being discussed with other people in the organization. The extensive consultation with senior managers, supervisors likely to enter the programme, and potential contributors is an essential factor in shaping the programme. Now the final touches have to be made to the programme to ensure it meets the needs identified by supervisors and their managers and can be delivered within existing time and resource constraints.

Contingency planning

This final check before launching the programme is to review the likelihood that it will work in practice, and see whether there are inherent defects that have to be attended to and overcome beforehand. In consulting those who are going to be affected by the programme we discover the hidden snags as they see them, and these insights are the ones that often point to problems we have been unable to see for ourselves. Consultation also discloses the best ways to tackle the obstacles, through the simple (but too often under-used) method of asking for help. When the programme has passed this final preview, it is ready to be put into effect.

Turning the programme into reality goes through a number of logical stages. Its duration has to be worked out and a block of time scheduled into the working year when there will be the best chance of signing up its participants. The other organizational events that have to take priority over training must be considered, such as the period around the end of the financial year or peak holiday periods.

A model schedule

Generally speaking, a block programme split into three separate periods of off-the-job training can cover a total of three or four months and be run twice a year, once in the period September to December and again in April to June. This avoids both the difficult period around March when budgets are being set and the peak holiday period around July and August. All scheduling has to be flexible until a pattern has been established which meets the needs of the majority, when it can be formalized in the training calendar.

It should be borne in mind that training programmes tend to develop their own momentum, and good training generates many demands for additional courses, workshops and one-off sessions which have to be fitted into the schedule. Many of these demands can be met if the training function plans to extend itself by actively promoting a programme to involve managers and supervisors as trainers. Naturally, these line managers will themselves need to be trained to undertake the training of others. Trainers will need to design a standard package of training techniques that managers can learn to apply to their staff when leading team-building and similar sessions of their own.

Leveraging training

Training managers to act in support of the training function is one of the most effective ways available to training specialists for leveraging human resource development into the organization. It will be seen later how valuable the involvement of supervisor trainers can be for extending vocational training to employees in the workplace.

After scheduling the programme, arrangements have to be made to advertise for candidates and set up the system for recruiting and selecting them. This part of the process of attracting candidates should be done in close co-operation with the line managers who will be their sponsors. It is especially important to involve sponsors at the inauguration of the programme, when the new system is not well understood and it is necessary for the trainer to take care that each step of the process of selection is carefully thought through and clarified.

Some sponsors will want to see that their supervisors take up as many places in the programme as possible. Other sponsors will be more reluctant to send supervisors off the job, arguing that they are more valuable at work. These are natural reactions which will have been anticipated, but both need to be dealt with in ways that comply with the ground-rules agreed for determining places.

Ground-rules for allocating participants to the programme

These will have included a comment on the need for the participants to be drawn from an equitable and balanced intake of applicants, taken from a wide cross-section of the supervisor population. There will not be places for everyone at the beginning, but the expectation is that the programme will run in the future, enabling all to be accommodated eventually. But only by making the first programme a success can this be assured. A successful launch is a key objective for trainers and sponsors alike: it is even more important for the development of the organization's managers of the future.

Application forms as market research tools

Advertisements for candidates that ask for applicants to complete a form will give selectors useful data to inform a decision on who attends. Personal data will be useful for programme registers, and the recording of job titles, length of service in the organization, time spent in the management role, and previous management training, can form the basis for establishing a permanent history of the evolving development programme.

Probably more valuable will be a section of the application form to be completed with a narrative on what prompted the individual to apply, what personal and organizational objectives they plan to fulfil, and which asks them to list what they consider to be the most pressing barriers they face in carrying out their job effectively. This section will give vital clues to the problems of line management that can be addressed in the programme.

Problems of supervisors

A careful categorizing of supervisors' problems identified in this way has found that they fall into three generic areas:

- personal problems caused by the individual's lack of knowledge about management and how to manage;
- interpersonal problems caused by the individual's inability to relate effectively to others, including the boss;
- organizational problems caused by lack of understanding of organizational procedures and systems.

Significant progress can be made to improve the calibre of supervisors by taking these topic areas as the starting-point for research to uncover the underlying causes of problems. The development programme can then be designed to seek solutions, and so provide specific support to improve the situation.

Trainers share the real world with their management colleagues. Both need to work together to attack the roots of management problems without getting into an over-complicated and time-consuming research programme to validate what they need to do. Effective development programmes are those which help managers to think their way around everyday problems and act accordingly.

The direct answers given in response to the simple questionnaire in the application form are perfectly capable of disclosing the pressing issues which are uppermost in the minds of supervisors. These are the issues that are of current concern to the supervisors. The solutions that have eluded them in the chaotic conditions of the workplace can often be found in the more favourable environment of the training programme.

Creative thinking techniques

The trainer's efforts to help supervisors solve their problems provide an ideal opportunity to introduce creative thinking techniques into the programme. For a nation reputed to be amongst the most innovative in the world, the United Kingdom has a considerable blind spot when it comes to widening access to creativity tools. The work of people like Edward de Bono, the exponent of lateral thinking, and Tony Buzan, formulator of the concept of Mind Mapping, ought to be a standard feature of management development programmes on a much greater scale than they are at present.

A recent initiative to introduce de Bono's Six Thinking Hats methodology to Civil Servants at the Department for Education and Employment was made at the instigation of the Department's Permanent Secretary, Michael Bichard. This is a long overdue recognition that we have better ways of using our minds than are commonly invoked, and it is interesting to speculate whether the attention shown by the Civil Service to these innovative techniques will lead to the more widespread use of them in the public service as a whole.

Writing the development programme

Whilst the selection process produces the audience for the programme, someone has to produce the script. The market research shows what managers' needs are, and gives trainers an idea of the programme materials, activities, seminars, sessions and workshops which are best suited to meet the needs. The next step is to identify the right mix of training resources that will best meet the needs of the course members.

There is rarely time to develop new materials and, in any case, training and development thrives on adapting what is already available and moulding it to the new training circumstances. Later it will be possible to design one's own original material, based on experience of what works. This is an important feature of the trainer's personal development which benefits the trainer and others working in the wider field of training. Most trainers acknowledge the importance of networking, and many reinforce its benefits by sharing the training materials they create.

Each topic of the development programme has to be studied and a learning plan made to set out the learning objectives to be achieved and how this will be done. The supply of learning materials is seemingly endless, as a study of the catalogues and brochures of training material providers will show.

However, most trainers have built up a repertoire of materials and techniques that they know will get results. These are the first choice, but only if they are relevant to the context in which they are to be applied. Case studies that relate to the running of a factory floor are not always seen to be relevant by public service managers attending a first-line training course. If all of their experience has been in the public sector, they will not take kindly to the observation that one of the outcomes of training is for them to be able to transfer their learning from one setting to another. Try to get some case study materials that show people at work in familiar settings, at least at the start of the development programme. Otherwise, you will risk obscuring the training message as people try to come to terms with an unaccustomed environment.

Involving all programme contributors in planning training

Training plans have to be decided in conjunction with the trainers who will lead each learning session. This is especially so when line managers are to be used in the programme. There are many good reasons for enlisting line managers, especially those at the top level, to take an active part in delivering the programme. Supervisors will gain invaluable insights into top management philosophy, and of the contribution they expect supervisors to make in leading the staff. The presentations give exceptional opportunities for supervisors to discuss plans and progress with their seniors. The commitment and motivation of supervisors is enhanced as senior managers share their thoughts about the organization and its future. Senior managers also are able to see their supervisors in a new light, and will begin to understand the importance of being involved in the development of this management resource.

Managers who are to be involved in training should be briefed on the part their presentation will play in the overall scheme of the programme. This calls for a meeting between trainer and manager, where the shape of the presentation can be firmed up and agreement reached on the kind of training materials, visual aids and other supporting materials required. Handouts relating to the key points of the presentation are always best issued at the end of the session. However, if issued during the session, the key points can form the headings of the talk, with space having been left on the paper for notes to be made.

The pre-programme briefing of the course presenters gives the trainer time to assess their ability and degree of confidence in taking on what is a somewhat daunting task to most people. This appraisal of trainer skills may discover gaps in experience that must be compensated. This fact has to be recognized and effective personal development provided in advance.

Train the trainers

A separate programme for training the trainers should be set up and run regularly so that an extensive pool of line managers with presentational skills can be created, and drawn on as required. The rationale for training managers is not only to enable the formal training resources of the organization to be reinforced, however. It is also important to provide managers with the training and communication skills that they can apply at the workplace.

Developing employees is one of the most important tasks of line managers. Line managers who are encouraged to gain training skills through the management development programme will find many opportunities to practise their presentational skills in the workplace. They will also become more proficient as they become part of the taskforce for developing the learning organization.

Remember that introducing any training approach which breaks new ground is a learning situation for trainers and they will need just as much support as others who are involved. The training team must take the initiative to establish its own form of self-development through mutual coaching and peer review.

Characteristics of trainers

NHS trainers can come from a variety of working backgrounds, but all will share certain characteristics in common with trainers from most other organizations. Foremost amongst these attributes is a keen interest in people. After all, the prime motivation of practitioners in human resource development is to help people to realize their potential. Along with this, trainers need to be technically competent and to know how to put over their message so that it is understood and acted on.

Trainers also need to be aware of what makes people behave in the way they do, and be able to help change the patterns of behaviour in themselves and in other people that are not achieving the results that count. They need to be well versed in interpersonal skills, good at communicating through the spoken and the written word, and conscientious in performing their duties.

Trainers do well if they are innovative, self-reliant and opportunistic – in the sense of being able to take advantage of and exploit opportunities that lead to the achievement of their training goals. Many trainers in the NHS and other public services have an entrepreneurial flair. This can be a useful trait to trainers, who need to run their functions with an emphasis on value for money and with a strong customer-service orientation.

Trainers are also learners

It is an advantage if a training team consciously commits each of its members to a programme of personal and professional development that is planned together as a part of a peer review and development process. This programme is specifically designed to ensure that mutual support is given to help individuals identify where they need to improve their contribution to the total training effort. Much of the success of the programme will depend on the degree of trust and support that can be generated between the team members, but this can be achieved over time if it is seen as an objective for the group.

Identifying where help and support are necessary comes out of the peer review process. The next stage of this self-help development programme is for team members to jointly agree how they will work together to achieve their planned individual improvements. This might entail some form of job rotation so that different members of the team have the opportunity to undertake new tasks, or to gain support from a more senior trainer in a training event so that they can observe and learn what is effective and what is not.

It is above all essential that the whole team cultivates a strong results focus, and learns from regular reviews of the outcomes of their learning programmes. Any trainer who sincerely wishes to excel will find that self-development will come from taking advantage of the learning opportunities that abound in the training world.

Mentors and mentoring

The role of the mentor is a key factor in the development of people. Mentoring is a kind of coaching, in which a more experienced colleague provides one-to-one support in the work setting. The aim is to establish the conditions for encouraging personal growth by providing advice derived from practical knowledge to meet obstacles encountered at work.

Mentoring is a key component of the supervisory programme and should be a part of the support given to all involved, whether trainees or trainers. The programme will need to involve senior managers as mentors from the outset to get them to share their hard-won experience with their supervisors.

Developing management skills is a challenging task and training resources are expensive, time-consuming and rarely available on the scale required to meet demand. This is especially so in health care settings where the political priority is to spend money on patients, generally to the exclusion of adequate training being given to managers who have to handle the human and systems management problems that arise. The use of in-house mentors to recycle their experience and augment the training resource is often neglected or under-used, yet it can be a cost-effective way of training.

Many companies in the private sector see the benefit of employing senior staff as mentors to give the benefit of their advice to young executives coming through the ranks. Some of these companies run internal mentoring programmes to ensure that they select and train the right mix of mentors who have the expertise and the right attitudes to make a difference. This is a system that has been adopted to good effect in some health care establishments and it has the potential to add a valuable extra dimension of effectiveness to in-house training programmes.

Mentoring is based on trust

Mentors have to impart their expertise to their client in an atmosphere of mutual trust, offering career-oriented advice and guidance to people to help them show measurable improvements in their working lives. Good interpersonal skills are needed, together with a genuine desire to find out the underlying problem that confronts the client by promoting the climate where the client knows it is safe to talk in confidence. The mentor also applies the spur by challenging present performance, helping the client to set improved targets and monitoring progress.

Mentoring programmes exist in the NHS in medical and nursing areas, and in professions allied to medicine, where peer support is a recognized method of passing on experience and overseeing standards of performance. High-fliers amongst the graduate intake to management schemes will also be part of a mentoring scheme.

In spite of these examples, it is still rare for a formal mentoring scheme to be a part of a supervisory development programme. Any serious attempt to develop supervisors should involve mentors to complement the basic training. Mentors keep abreast of the new knowledge and skills that need to be passed on and absorbed by their supervisors, and can ensure that they apply these in their practical work on return to their jobs.

At the outset of the new supervisory development programme, efforts need to be made to promote strong links with the managers responsible for them. This is an important part of the marketing and selling stage to promote the idea of transforming supervisors and will establish a valuable network of connections with senior managers. Trainers can encourage senior managers to be mentors by reminding them that they will gain a direct benefit by improving the calibre of the supervisors in their departments.

Sponsors as mentors

It is likely that the first wave of mentors will be found amongst the sponsoring managers to whom the supervisors in the programme report. Experience has shown that this method of self-selection may not always be the best, as it may not be possible to match mentors to supervisors to ensure compatibility in the different roles that each will play in the mentoring programme.

It may be found that some managers have difficulty in relating to the essentially supportive and teaching role required of the mentor, especially when dealing with their own supervisor. Where this is recognized beforehand, it should be possible for the trainer to discuss the problem with both parties to see if there is any way of putting the supervisor with another mentor. This will be difficult to address if the manager expects to be the mentor. The situation will have to be watched closely to see that it is working, and the initial briefing that will be given to mentors can refer to the possibility of relationship issues getting in the way of effective mentoring.

Training mentors for supervisory development

Expect to allow for a short training programme for mentors well before the actual supervisory programme is launched. There needs to be enough time between these two events for the messages in the mentor training to be understood and acted on. Feedback from the managers has to be collected and considered and any questions arising answered before the trainer briefs the supervisors on the role of the mentor. The mentor training session need not be long, but it does need to cover all the most pressing issues that will concern managers who are to undertake what is probably a new role.

As in the supervisory development programme itself, the content of mentor training has to reflect the expectations and needs of the managers who are selected to be mentors. Some preparatory research will be undertaken with these potential mentors to establish their views on what they understand the role will entail: how feasible they feel it will be to act as a mentor; how they propose to carry out the task; and what sort of standards they will require to measure their success.

Managers' perceptions of mentoring

Answers that have been given to these questions when they were put in a telephone interview were illuminating, and are quite probably representative of the views of many managers when confronted with what they may consider to be yet another imposition on their limited time. Here is what we were told.

- Most managers are not sure what a mentor is, or how to go about being one.
- Many will question the relevance of mentoring someone they see every day.
- Others will say they act as mentors already.
- Some will say they do not need to be trained.
- Others have reservations about the value of putting time into helping their supervisor.

Often the reason for these reactions is that the mentoring process is new to them and consequently it is natural to resist change. Sometimes there is genuine resistance to it, on the grounds that they have never been mentored themselves, and what was good enough for them should be good enough for others. All of these responses will help the trainer work out the kind of training session that will deal not only with the factual information that mentors require, but also can help to dispel any underlying negativity to the introduction of mentoring for supervisors.

Assumptions for training

When the trainer is considering the development of a training programme two assumptions have to be kept in mind, for they provide the dynamic for the design of the programme. One is that the programme will result in development taking place in the people concerned, that is, something that was latent will evolve, in this case the potential of the individual. The second assumption is that this change will take place within a planned course of study, and because of it.

These requirements set parameters for the design by providing two essential themes to be pursued by the programme designers – personal growth and the time-scale in which it takes place. Other assumptions will be made: for example, that the content of the programme will be sufficiently rigorous and appropriate, that the participants will have the capacity and motivation to learn, and that the trainers will be able to overcome all obstacles preventing the successful completion of the programme. There are dangers in assuming too much, as there are in assuming too little. Perhaps the most positive assumption to make is that the programme will exceed the expectations of participants, and then work unremittingly to make sure that happens.

Building on market research

Market research will have been carried out at an earlier stage to discover the knowledge, skills and attitudes that supervisors needed to learn and practise if they were to be more competent in their role. Now the results of this research can be analysed to identify the common needs applying to the majority so that training resources can be allocated to deal with priorities. What goes into the programme will be specifically designed to meet those needs. Whilst every group of supervisors will give different weighting and priority to their needs, there is a good deal of experience to suggest that two broad fields exist where supervisors in general feel they lack support. They need to know about their organization, and they need to know about their role within it.

A development programme that aims to raise understanding and awareness of the organization, its systems and the 'way things are done around here' and, in addition, gives supervisors a sense of their identity within the management team, will be of value in most organizations, and especially in those beset by rapid changes, such as the NHS and associated public services.

Supervisors need to know more about the organization in which they work because they want to feel they are an essential part of the total management team. Their feeling of confidence in their role depends on senior managers giving them enough information about the organization's plans to enable them to lead effectively. Supervisors who do not know where the organization is going will not be able to take others towards organizational objectives.

The role of senior managers

It is always preferable for senior managers to be part of a planned system of communications that allows for regular updating on plans and progress. The development programme can provide the opportunity for senior managers to consider what information their supervisors should have and give it to them when they are at their most receptive. The development programme is where senior managers can display leadership, act as mentors and strengthen communication links within the management team. They will be able to speak with authority based on their position as leaders of supervisors, but the content of their contribution should follow clear guidelines if it is to fit into the overall design of the development programme.

A two-stage guideline for contributors

Guidelines for the programme contributors are a natural extension of the programme's learning objectives. Every contribution, whether lecture, planned reading, group discussion or personal development activity needs to be considered as a part of a jigsaw. Everything associated with the development programme is connected with everything else. At the end, if the big picture that emerges is to replicate the original vision conceived for the programme, then the design of each part cannot be left to chance.

Just as travellers need signposts to show the way over unknown territory, so directions have to be given to programme tutors, especially if the subject matter is new, as it will be in the case of a new supervisory programme. These guidelines spell out in detail the purpose of each component part of the programme and indicate how they fit into the overall learning scheme.

Guideline stage 1

It will be seen that a guideline has two sections. In the first section, the guideline should explain the general framework of the development programme, describe the purpose and state how the stages of the programme will lead to that goal. It should be possible to outline this section on no more than one sheet of A4 paper (preferably less), and this statement of intent needs to be formulated by the entire team of trainers, including the line managers who have been selected to contribute to the programme. This general programme outline has to capture the essential what, why and how of the programme, succinctly and memorably. It will be the opening section of all the guidelines that will subsequently be produced for contributors.

Guideline stage 2

The second phase of producing a contributor's guideline focuses on the content of the particular session that is to be delivered. This will take account of the learning outcomes to be achieved, state the training materials and resources that are available, give details of the time, place and accessibility of presentational aids, and provide contributors with an offer of assistance in planning their session. Programme development has to be monitored by the trainer at all stages to ensure that the planned contributions will meet set standards, but there is a particular requirement to oversee how contributors plan to put the guidelines into effect.

The trainer should therefore meet contributors face to face to finalize their approach and to establish – as diplomatically as may be necessary – if the planned session has been prepared effectively or whether the contributor could benefit from help in designing the presentation. When all the sessions have been planned, they can be previewed by the group of managers and supervisors who took part in the preliminary discussions to specify the programme content and methodology. In this way, those stakeholders who were involved in the planning stage can now – as we saw in Chapter 5 – be brought together for a final overview of the programme.

Standards of achievement for measuring progress

A development programme is a vehicle for arriving at preplanned learning outcomes, enabling participants to perform more effectively as they apply the new learning they acquire. Progress to meet these goals has to be measured, and this is where standards are needed to provide the yardsticks of attainment. Standards are necessary for participants and trainers so that both can measure how effectively they are meeting their own learning and development goals, either in providing the learning or in applying it.

Measuring progress should be a continuing process throughout the development programme, with regular opportunities being provided when candidates can reflect on the lessons learned and share their various insights with the trainer and each other. These periods help the trainer to judge whether the messages are getting across and the work being put into the learning process is bearing fruit. This is valuable feedback, which should be a basis for improving the programme where this is found to be necessary.

Measuring progress is also important to the candidates and some systematic means should be made available to enable them to record their achievements on the programme. Introducing managers to the principles of continuous self-development should be a regular feature of the development programme. The aim is to encourage all those involved in the programme to become familiar with the principles of lifelong learning and introduce them to the practice of continuing self-development as an intrinsic part of their working life.

Building on self-development

Managers who use a systematic method of planned self-development throughout the programme will be able to carry this over into their working life after the formal development programme ends. It will give them a learning tool with which to construct a personal development centre in their own workplace and to maintain the momentum of their own development.

We should not underestimate the sense of anticlimax that often affects people when they leave a demanding development programme. In the programme they have been involved – sometimes for the first time in their lives – in the process of achieving previously unrealized levels of personal growth. Development programmes should provide something extra to enable managers to capitalize on this awareness, and this can be achieved by making continuing development an intrinsic part of the programme.

One way of doing this is to include continuing personal and professional development in the syllabus. Time should be set aside in the development programme to promote the idea of self-development over a series of sessions, in which managers will discuss and clarify the principles, gain understanding of the process, and work out an acceptable methodology to apply continuing development as a follow-up to the programme.

It is often helpful when introducing changes to outline the benefits that the individual stands to gain from the change. Introducing a continuing development process as though it were a chore to be undertaken by managers in addition to their normal work is not likely to inspire enthusiasm.

Appeal to enlightened self-interest

The picture is often different and can be made more appealing by concentrating on the benefits that continuous personal and professional development brings with it. There are undoubted benefits in making this development a feature of any management growth programme. Some of these benefits will have been brought out in discussions with managers who were being introduced to the concept, and are set out here for others who may contemplate making continuing development a feature of their development programmes.

Perhaps the biggest benefit is to get managers to understand and accept that ongoing personal development will be an essential feature of the training and development schemes that the organization will offer in the future. This is likely to happen as the emphasis on lifelong learning takes hold as a consequence of the emerging national educational and economic development strategy.

Continuing personal and professional development

Here are some reasons for making continuing personal development (CPD) an integral part of supervisory management development:

- CPD underlines the message that development is a personal responsibility.
- CPD builds on learning achieved in the development programme.
- CPD maintains the motivation to keep up to date with new thinking in management.
- CPD improves capacity to innovate through actively seeking creative ways to solve workplace problems.
- CPD uses the working environment as a learning venue.
- CPD positions the supervisor as an exemplar, able to influence employees to adopt a lifetime learning approach.

The personal development plan

The trainer must design a methodology to assist each supervisor to draw up a personal development plan that will be worked on until the end of the formal training period. The purpose of personal development is to ensure that the individual first identifies a behaviour that needs to be changed in order to improve personal effectiveness. This requirement immediately places two responsibilities on the supervisor. The first is to reflect on what personal characteristics, attitudes, skills or areas of knowledge are inadequate and need to be rectified. The second is to assume accountability for changing themselves. They have to identify their personal need to change, and do something about it.

Their personal development comes out of their search to change the way they behave as managers. The learning outcome will be defined and measured by their ability to act in a different way after they have fulfilled their development plan. We have seen that the learning is consolidated by recording the stages of the behavioural change in a portfolio of learning. The act of committing the process to writing provides more than a chronology of the process. It establishes a record of achievement – an opportunity to reflect on the lessons learned, and so reinforce the learning process.

The learning log

The entry into the portfolio can be made by completing a separate learning log, which itself need not be elaborate. There are a number of learning logs on the market, but it is possible, and probably more effective, to get a group of managers to design one that is suitable for their needs. In-house learning logs do not need to be sophisticated, and can be less expensive than commercial versions. Producing their own will give managers a better understanding of the purpose of the learning log, and because it has been developed by themselves will be more likely to be accepted.

A perfectly adequate learning log can consist of one side of a sheet of A4 paper, divided into four sections. The first section provides space for the learner to identify the event or experience that provided the learning experience. The second section captures the reflections that have been made when considering what lessons were learned. The third section describes the next steps that will enable the learner to build on the learning gained, and what is to be done to put this into effect. The last section of the log describes what happened as a result of that further action. This then leads on to a different set of experiences, which can in turn be treated as further learning opportunities.

Experiential learning

This learning log is modelled on the learning cycle developed by David Kolb and others. Kolb, writing in *Experiential Learning*,

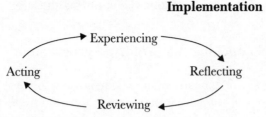

Figure 8.1   The Kolb Learning Cycle

defined learning as 'the process whereby knowledge is created through the transformation of experience'. He proposed that people learn in stages, which he termed the learning cycle. The incentive to learn comes from the drive to develop, which is common to humans. When we are impelled into an experience, which can be of our own making or the result of events over which we have no control, we are given the opportunity to reflect on it and consider why and how the experience happened in the way it did. We may be led to review the circumstances leading to our having the experience and propose ways of doing it differently. By taking action in line with these new ideas, we transform the original experience into something different.

If the new experience is judged to place us nearer to a desired goal we have for ourselves, then it will be counted as successful and the actions that induced it may be repeated until they become a habit. If the new experience was not successful, we have the opportunity to reflect on it with a view to taking different action in the future. Either way, we have gained knowledge by transforming our experience, and therefore have 'learned'.

Good results in personal development can be achieved with the most basic of learning tools. What counts above all is that supervisors clearly understand and accept the purpose of the exercise, are motivated by the benefits they will get from being involved in it, and enthusiastically take it on because they are convinced it will help them in their careers. Personal development will be an integral feature of the overall supervisory development programme, along with mentoring, and will need to be carefully explained in the initial briefing session that precedes the full programme.

Launching the prototype programme

The launch of the programme is analogous to the launch of a new model of car. The programme is a learning vehicle and it is going to be tested for faults under highly critical eyes. It makes sense for the trainer to use the prototype stage to enrol the first wave of candidates to check whether the programme design, training materials, learning experiences and the way the programme is conducted meet expectations. The programme is centred on the theme of continuous development. It must practise what it teaches by enabling trainers to learn how it can be improved and making sure those improvements become future practice.

CHAPTER 9

The project stage, part 1

The project stage is the final part of the supervisory development programme, preceded by two theoretical stages (outlined below). It is the most important because it brings together all three strands of the training process. This stage enables participants to practise the skills developed in the first two stages and apply their new-found expertise to resolve a problem of concern to the organization. The project is where individual and organizational development combine to gain added value from the programme.

The project consolidates theory and practice into learning. Candidates learn as a team to apply their experience, knowledge and skills to manage a problem or situation, and to do this under conditions that replicate the pressures they encounter in their normal work environment. The value of the project method lies in the opportunity it gives for each team member to learn how to handle the interpersonal dynamics of the group as well as to share in all the management actions required to plan and resource the project work and deliver the required outcomes.

The theoretical underpinning of the programme

In the full three-stage supervisory development programme, the first two stages deal with theory. During these stages the supervisor learns about the management of the organization in the widest sense, but with special reference to the importance of the supervisory role in the hierarchy of management. This is the part of the programme where the course members can explore new ideas about management, and be given insights into the classic techniques of supervision that continue to get results in dealing with the organizational and personal issues which will continue to face the supervisor in the modern setting.

In these first two weeks, the supervisor is given the opportunity to detach from the real pressures of the workplace and begin the slow but necessary process of considering in some depth what needs to be done to make a difference to the way the practice of supervision is carried out. In this consideration, the course members will be encouraged to let their imagination conceive of better and more effective systems and practices that could be introduced to replace the outmoded ones which they know are not working as they should. This phase of the programme can be one of the most important for changing attitudes and preparing the supervisor to contemplate the possibility that lasting change will be an outcome of the programme.

An academic input is made into the programme to impart knowledge, but theory is not enough. Learning is recognized when the learner can demonstrate the ability to do something with greater competence than hitherto. The first step is to assess the candidate's current understanding of management, however elementary this may be. This provides the baseline for adding new, necessary and relevant information which will enable the candidate to reach the level of knowledge required to handle the organizational and personal problems that will be met in the new management role.

Once the theory has been imparted and is understood, the initial groundwork will have been done to prepare the candidate for the third, or project, stage of the programme. This can now be entered into with confidence, and candidates can take practical steps to build on the theoretical underpinning as they go forward to make their management role more effective.

Practical application of knowledge, skills and understanding

The project is an intense learning experience where practical management skills are demonstrated and tested. It also provides the setting in which supervisors can experience a powerful learning model that they can later use to transform their own workplace into a learning centre for developing their teams. The same procedures and techniques that are used in the project stage are ideally suited for use in the workplace, simply because they direct learning towards the resolution of immediate problems and get results that improve the quality of working life. This irresistible combination of benefits actually motivates people to participate in working together for mutual advantage.

Combining individual and group projects

A project can allow management skills to be demonstrated either on an individual basis, through the medium of a personal project, or on a team basis by setting a project for a group of supervisors. Both methods are practised in this programme. During the theoretical stage, assignments, or mini-projects, are set to enable individuals to show how they understand and apply the knowledge component of the programme. The main project is preferred for developing effective teamwork.

Mini-projects, or assignments, should be introduced widely into the academic stages of the programme to reinforce the learning of new concepts and to enable supervisors to work out how they might use this knowledge to make their jobs more effective.

Individual assignments

Assignments differ from the team projects in being carried out entirely by the individual supervisor. They have the status of mini-projects and need to be planned and followed through as methodically as the main project stage. Some reasons why these individual assignments are important are:

- They demonstrate that theory can be transferred into practice.
- They reinforce the learning cycle by providing a stage for reflection.
- They provide a record of development that can be reviewed later.
- They give feedback to the individual.
- They give written evidence that programme objectives have been met.

Assignment stage 1: Theory

Take the case of an assignment set on the topic of recruitment and selection. In the theoretical stage, the supervisor would be taken through the recruitment process to gain an overall understanding of the joint roles and responsibilities for recruitment that are shared between the supervisor and the personnel function. The review would aim to give a thorough understanding of how the recruitment process is carried out in the organization, and would pay particular attention to the role of the supervisor in this. The supervisor must be conversant with recruitment policy, such as the impact of employment law on actions taken during the selection stage. In this connection the implications of equal opportunity legislation, and much more that was hitherto the preserve of the personnel function, is finding its way increasingly into the supervisor's remit.

A grasp of the logistical factors entailed in recruitment might entail having a knowledge of how to review the need for recruiting a replacement for a vacant post or whether remaining jobs can be restructured. If the vacancy is not to be filled, how will the supervisor go about reassigning and retraining existing employees and deciding how to apply any necessary reward to compensate for additional or higher-level work? If the recruitment is to proceed, the supervisor must be able to draw up a job and person specification, and know all the implications involved in advertising, shortlisting, interviewing and inducting the new employee into the workplace. All this is part of the 'classroom' component of training and will be recorded in the learning log.

Assignment stage 2: Practice

The assignment is concluded when the supervisor has carried out a recruitment in real terms and has been able to draw conclusions from reflecting on the total process. These reflections, which might indicate how the process could have been improved, will be written up and attached to the initial assignment as a supplementary learning record. This position may be reached only at some point in the future, but the training programme should require it to be done even if some time elapses before the supervisor is able to participate in a recruitment exercise. Only by insisting on preserving this continuity will the ultimate benefits of the training be realized.

Individual assignments and group projects compared

Some external qualifying bodies consider that a solo project is better suited to proving the contribution of an individual, and there is no doubt that individual project work is important and should be recognized. However, the organization is the sum of all individual contributions and, in the project stage, team effort is stressed as the primary means to achieve corporate goals.

The team project is a microcosm of the way the organization itself works. It underlines the need for participants to learn how to work together, to set attainable objectives, to co-operate and share their personal resources, and to subjugate the natural desire for self-distinction to the greater good of the team. In practice, the synergy of teamwork will always produce results that are greater than the sum of the individual contributions.

Action learning in supervisory development

Team projects are based on the concept of action learning, a practical learning methodology that is ideally suited to the development of management. Essentially a problem-solving technique for teams, action learning was given prominence by the radical management thinker Reg Revans who, though disclaiming primary authorship of the concept, nevertheless codified its principles and has been its primary protagonist for more than half a century.

Action learning has an interesting history in the National Health Service. It was introduced by Revans in the 1960s to study the effect of staff morale on patient care. That research was financed by the Nuffield Provincial Hospitals Trust 'to probe more deeply the impression that the hospital with good personal relations and freedom from an unduly rigid system of hierarchy is also able to keep its staff and to help its patients towards a quicker recovery'. It says much for the intractable nature of the organization that this hypothesis is as much in need of research and resolution today as it was three decades ago.

Further action learning work followed in the NHS with the launch of the Hospital Internal Communication Project, under the auspices of the King Edward Hospital Fund for London (the King's Fund) and the then Department of Health and Social Security. Since then, action learning has become a mainstream management development medium on an international scale. Trainers and others requiring further background to the action learning process are referred to the copious writings on the subject held in the Revans Centre for Action Learning and Research of the University of Salford, England.

The ideas of action learning have especial relevance to the use of project work for developing supervisors, though Revans does consider that some forms of project work do not meet his criteria as vehicles for action learning. He is averse to project work which, in his words, is set up by 'higher management' to form 'a working party to make recommendations about some trouble it has detected' and to make 'recommendations for others to implement'. He is particularly dismissive of the project team that tries 'to find out what their principals are ready to accept rather than what the problem really is, let alone how to get effective action taken about it'.

On these grounds, purists may argue that not all the essential features of an action learning programme are incorporated in the approach used in the development programme described here, especially if project teams are not allowed to put into effect their best recommendations. There is some justification for this view at the start of a project-based development programme. Initially, senior managers may not be wholly convinced of the importance of giving their supervisory teams scope to change the way the organization works. However, as the programmes develop over time and more and more good ideas emerge from the project teams, the tendency amongst progressive senior managers is to allow action learners to implement their innovations. This marks a significant shift in top management thinking that will have far-reaching consequences for organizational and personal development. It can be one of the first signs that the organizational mind-set is shifting, however tentatively, towards empowerment.

Essential objectives of action learning

However, the project stage of this development programme includes sufficient of the Revans action learning assumptions to justify calling it action learning. In particular, the programme incorporates the following three essential objectives cited by Revans in *The ABC of Action Learning*, his review of 25 years of experience.

According to Revans, the objectives of action learning are:

- To make useful progress on the treatment of some problem (opportunity) in an enterprise.
- To give sufficient scope to a participant to find out how best to approach an ill-defined problem to which nobody knows the solution or has even an appropriate course of action.
- To enable management developers, in partnership with senior management, to contrive an environment in which all

managers can learn with and from each other in the pursuit of their common tasks.

Any organization that seriously pursues these objectives is on the way to becoming an authentic 'learning organization'. To build up and build on the potential of employees and to use their energy to search for opportunities for growth in their daily work are characteristics of growing organizations.

Internal resources + external conditions = synergy

One of the premises of action learning (which it shares with neuro-linguistic programming, although Revans recognized and stated it first) is that managers already have within themselves all the resources they need to tackle organizational problems. There is one external factor, however, that has to be provided by the organization – a culture that supports and encourages innovation and the freedom to put ideas into effect.

Managers may bring their experience, knowledge, skills and a desire to achieve, but this is not enough if the organization stops them from implementing their solutions. Organizations introducing action learning have to provide a supportive culture if the process is to take root.

The project stage of the supervisory development programme is the acid test which determines whether the organizational culture is receptive to action learning, and a study of the reactions of senior managers to the efforts of their supervisors will show whether attitudes to change are indeed becoming more responsive at the senior level.

Setting up the project stage

Assigning team members and identifying problems

A well-conducted action learning project starts by setting up teams and allocating them a problem that they are required to resolve through their own resources. At the beginning they need to be fully briefed on the principles of action learning. Although Revans has stated that the principles of action learning are so simple 'it takes an intellectual ten years thoroughly to misunderstand them', this simplicity can be a source of concern to some managers who have been raised on a diet of management nostrums whose complexities have been mistaken for profundity.

Briefing senior managers

Senior managers to whom the supervisors report should be included in the briefing on action learning given to the project teams. They are joint partners in the development programme and managers and supervisors need to know what action learning is about, and how they can all play a part in making this stage of the supervisor's development a success.

Management developers must take the lead in preparing senior managers for an active part in the project stage. This means that the trainer will need to brief senior managers on the purpose of the project stage, pointing out that it is about practical change management at the operational level and that the organization (and consequently the senior management) have a stake in the outcomes.

Roles of senior managers

Senior managers as tutors

Senior managers have several roles in the development programme. We have seen that they are extremely important as lecturers to supervisors during the academic phases of the programme. It is always valuable to involve managers in sharing appropriate, relevant, up-to-date information about the organizational mission, objectives and goals with their own supervisors. Only managers can have the depth of knowledge of these issues to be able to put them across in a way that raises awareness and enthusiasm in their supervisors and helps them to understand what the organization has to do. By communicating this knowledge, managers enhance their leadership status.

It will be recalled that work will have been done by the trainer at the programme-planning stage, in discussions with senior managers, to identify potential internal lecturers. Their selection as lecturers will have been followed up with a full briefing on the purpose and content of their session, and trainers can help to structure the presentation if requested. Certainly, visual aids and handouts will have to be specified and help may be needed to produce these to meet the standards set for the programme.

In addition to their involvement as course lecturers, there are several important roles for senior managers throughout the project stage. The first is to work with the trainer to agree criteria for identifying practical problems.

Senior managers as problem-setters

It is essential that the senior managers are closely involved in setting the problems that the action learning teams will resolve. In particular, the problems should be selected with the following criteria in mind:

- The problems must be real and be familiar to the participants.
- The problems should be capable of being resolved in the timeframe allocated to this stage.
- The recommended solution should show that it will save money.
- The solution should out-perform existing practice.
- The solution should lead to a valuable operational improvement.
- The solution should be capable of being tested in a small-scale prototype, or pilot scheme, preferably under the ongoing management of the project team involved.
- The solution should be readily transferable to other problem areas.

It is of little use to manufacture an imaginary issue to be resolved. Even the most cursory consideration will expose plenty of real problems that are impeding organizational performance, and many of these can be dealt with by a team motivated by the prospect of having their success recognized by their peers and senior managers.

Project teams in management development programmes are a highly efficient way of using resources. Their motivation and commitment invariably gives a substantial return on the cost of their training and, by using them to introduce practical improvements, the organization gains substantial benefits.

Senior managers as project team champions

Another role for senior managers is to support the work of the teams. A nominated manager, or managers, should be available to each team to discuss progress, offer advice and constructive criticism, point out potential conflicts of interest between the team and non-participating workgroups, and encourage creative problem-solving to overcome obstacles.

These are essentially coaching skills and trainers will do well to explore the need to set up workshops in these skills for senior managers. This is a further example of the training spin-off that emanates from any in-house development programme. We have seen that the further training of supervisors as work-based trainers increases the capacity of the organization by enabling them to develop employees. Similarly, by extending coaching skills more widely amongst senior managers, trainers make it possible for better coaching and mentoring to be practised in the organization. The supervisory development programme is a hub from which all kinds of complementary training programmes spin off.

Senior managers as resource managers

Senior managers are quick to recognize the benefits of setting projects to be tackled by their supervisory teams. They are being provided with the resources of a team of supervisors to resolve a problem that would not otherwise be resolved. The scope for improvement is wide. Issues to be dealt with could include the need to review how existing policies are being implemented, what should be done to introduce new practices in the light of changes in legislation, or whether to introduce different training approaches, for instance, by amending employee induction procedures.

Successful projects have been conducted within a wide range of areas, of which the following are a few examples. Research and Recommendations for change have been made as a result of projects which investigated patients' waiting times, optimum ambulance-routing schedules, noise-abatement schemes in hospitals, the design and development of staff restaurant facilities, and the quality of care provided to clients.

In all of these situations it was possible to change prevailing situations for the better, but resolving problems is only the most obvious benefit of the programme. The project stage also helps senior managers to recognize the potential of supervisors by highlighting their hidden talents. This provides data to inform management succession plans, and many supervisors who have been promoted to higher echelons of management have come to prominence as a result of the contribution they have made to the project.

Senior managers as organizers of learning

The preparatory period, in which management developers discuss these issues with senior line managers, provides an ideal platform from which to attain one of the three action learning objectives cited earlier. This period is when trainers and managers can jointly set about to contrive the conditions in which managers can learn with and from each other in the pursuit of their common tasks.

The time spent in presenting the business case for using action learning as a tool for training supervisors can be highly profitable for a management developer who seeks to influence senior managers to recognize that organizational development begins with people. Trainers will also find that their influence on decision-makers will be greatly enhanced if they can develop a programme that is able to combine to good effect the twin issues of personal development and organizational development. Action learning is able to get results that make a real difference in both of these areas.

Clarifying the project

When the problems to be addressed by the teams have been identified in broad terms, they need to be fine tuned so they can be written down. They may have to go through a number of written drafts before they are sufficiently comprehensive and unambiguous to allocate to the teams. Even then, teams may still find they have to talk through the terms of reference with the manager who has been nominated to act as their mentor. Once the supervisory team is clear on what is expected, it is ready to enter the action planning phase of the project.

Senior managers as project overseers

The active commitment of senior managers has to continue throughout the project stage because they are as involved in the attainment of action learning objectives as are the team members, and have to be seen to establish an effective learning environment. Inevitably, the project stage attracts the interest of the senior managers who act as sponsors to the various teams. They feel they have a proprietary interest to check that the way the problem is dealt with will reflect as much on themselves as on the prowess of the team itself. This can lead managers to propose their own remedies to the team and try to mould the outcome into what they feel will fit with the organization.

A word of warning

Senior managers like to oversee the development of the project. They believe they are helping but in fact they may be subconsciously seeking to preserve the status quo and avoid the possibility that the project will get into risky areas where new thinking will challenge the old order of things. Unfortunately, this attitude is inimical to the spirit of development. Discouraging the project team from searching for new solutions, some of which may not appear immediately acceptable but which may contain the seed of a long overdue breakthrough, merely perpetuates the unsatisfactory present position by inhibiting initiative.

Team members must be given the freedom to seek their own path to a solution by combining their insights and wisdom, sharpened by 'insightful questioning' of the circumstances in which they find themselves.

Trainers should also try to avoid too much interference with the work of teams and encourage their senior management colleagues to give project teams their head. If action learning is constrained, it will not deliver powerful results.

CHAPTER 10

The project stage, part 2

Planning and managing the project stage requires that two points be borne in mind. First, the purpose of the project is to improve the way the organization works by applying the energy of a motivated team to change current practice. Second, the project provides an environment for innovation. It is the aim of the development programme to integrate these two requirements to the advantage of both the individuals and the organization. The twin outcomes of an effective project will be a recognizable change in the way the organization deals with a problem, and evidence that the change was brought about by members of a team who learned how to achieve that result as part of a planned exercise in personal development.

The organization's senior managers will have identified the problems to be resolved. It is now necessary to assign the members of the development programme to smaller teams to manage the project stage. The task is to create teams with members from different functions who will be able to bring a wide range of experiences and perspectives to bear upon the project task they are assigned.

Assigning supervisors to project teams

Supervisors need to be formed into project teams that bring together people from widely different functional backgrounds. This is to ensure that there is a rich and diverse mix of experience that can be brought to bear on the problem that needs to be resolved. The act of harmonizing each individual's approach to problem-solving and focusing their energies to achieve a common approach gives the team members an insight into the challenges of managing across functional boundaries. The process is very effective in breaking down inter-departmental barriers to co-operation. Lessons learned in this context have been found to be of great value to supervisors who later have to achieve change in their place of work.

Allocating individuals to teams will be simplified if the trainer can draw from a full course membership that has been selected to include representatives from a wide range of professions and workplaces within the organization.

Other issues, such as logistics, education balance and resources also affect how the course membership is divided. How these were dealt with in one health authority, comprising five units of management, is considered next.

Logistics

At the start of the programme logistical and educational reasons were considered, such as the number of potential candidates that could be accommodated, the likelihood of their being released from duty to attend the programme, the accessibility to them of the central training location where the theoretical study components of the programme would be held, and the training resources available to handle all stages of the programme. The nature of the catchment area with its five separate units dictated that there would have to be some form of proportional representation to ensure that each unit had an equitable distribution of places on the programme. This fitted in ideally with the plan to focus the training on action learning teams, and meant that the numbers of supervisors in each unit team could be predetermined and balanced between the main functions in each unit.

The initial exercise to market the new programme had given a clear indication that there would be a great demand for places, but this had to be balanced against the availability of in-house trainers and the requirement to reduce spending on external training providers. The fact that the programme was very much a prototype to be tested and improved in the light of experience meant that it presented a learning curve for trainers as much as for supervisors.

Training resources determine programme size

The training resource issue finally determined programme size. It was decided to arrange two intakes annually for supervisors who were already in post, had been appointed in the past five years (the majority having had no formal training in the role) and who needed to update their capability. These were to form the core group. Entry into each intake group was restricted to twenty participating supervisors. Earlier market research had shown that the programme should ultimately aim to cover three categories of manager, each with different needs that reflected their position in the management hierarchy. In addition to the recently pro-moted, there was a large population of individuals who aspired to become supervisors. This group was expected to increase as they identified with role models who had successfully completed the new development programmes and who would encourage others to follow them. The third group consisted of senior managers, especially those who became interested in and closely associated with the emerging culture of learning. They were keen to extend their own professional development and to show by their example that they supported the learning initiative.

The strategy was that an action learning-based programme as has been described would form the initial plank in the total management development structure. Other programmes would be added in time, but the imperative was to gain credibility and experience by running one course successfully. This decision allowed trainers and the organization as a whole to come to terms with the introduction of a new management development approach, and to avoid the danger of becoming over-extended.

The supervisory profile

Market research had also shown that half of the total population of supervisory candidates were in the nursing profession, with the remainder in administration, including finance, supplies, works, and domestic and hotel service functions, and professionals supplementary to medicine, such as ambulance personnel, and those in physiotherapy and other patient services. This model can be adopted by other health care organizations to suit their own circumstances. If the object is to design a programme on similar lines, candidates should be drawn from a variety of professions and departments. This will maximize the benefits that come from developing supervisors in multi-functional teams.

Balancing the intake

To keep to the planned intake of twenty, it was decided to allocate four places to each of the five units of management. Of these, two candidates were from nursing and the rest from the other services. Each unit-based team was to be the focus group to take on a project centred on that particular unit, but in the classroom stages before the project stage commenced they were required to mix closely with their colleagues from other units, even to the extent of sitting next to a different member of the course every day.

Selecting candidates and researching development needs

Just as the project was identified by locality management, so the selection of candidates was their responsibility, in each case assisted by the training manager. Broad criteria for selection were agreed in discussion with managers, mainly aimed at ensuring some minimum entry standards around which to design the content of the course. This led to the recording of entry standards by length of service in a supervisory capacity, extent and kind of any previous management training, identification of personal objectives for attending the programme, listing of current management problems being experienced, and listing of three pressing development needs that were adversely affecting their present performance.

This pre-programme review became the basis for an ongoing research programme conducted in the training department, which enabled training sessions to be targeted to the changing needs of supervisors. In addition, this feedback from the line management markedly assisted trainers to keep in touch with the changing aspirations of supervisors and to be aware of the way organizational policy affects those who have a prime responsibility for its operation.

The selection criteria were agreed with line managers during consultation at the programme design stage, and aimed to give senior managers and potential candidates the opportunity to sit down together and decide who were eligible to go into the programme, and who would have either to wait until they met the entry requirements or a place became available. Many had to be deferred to a later programme, and trainers were able to advise nominating managers of plans for a series of short, taster training sessions that would be run to give deferred supervisors the chance to brush up their understanding of management issues and so improve their chances of being selected for the main programme in future. This is an example of the multiplier effect in training, where the original innovation of a core development programme leads to a proliferation of associated training activity.

The learning contract

When a candidate was selected, the nominating manager began the process of working out a learning contract in discussion with the supervisor to suit their particular needs. The learning contract was one of a number of innovations tested when the new supervisor training programme was introduced. It had several main uses.

Learning contract for promoting learning partnership

In the first place the contract was introduced as part of an experiment to test out new ideas for integrating managers, supervisors and trainers more closely together as partners in the learning process. Strengthening communications between manager and supervisor in this way was seen to be a desirable by-product of the development programme. Any opportunity to have manager and supervisor sit down and discuss their mutual expectations of the development programme was seen to be a step towards promoting better communications.

Learning contract to encourage mentoring

The learning contract also helps improve communication by formalizing the process of enlisting senior managers as guides and mentors to the supervisors undertaking the training. Discussing the purpose of the learning contract opens a useful dialogue between managers and trainers on mentoring, which leads to the introduction of training sessions in mentoring and coaching techniques for managers. Managers feel they have a greater stake in the development of their supervisory colleagues, and learn that training is not only a responsibility for trainers but is theirs as well.

Learning contract as agreement to learn

The learning contract begins with a declaration of the training mission, making it the central focus for the learning agreement that follows. It goes on to spell out the individual responsibilities of each of the parties to the contract, that is, the sponsoring manager, the supervisor, and the trainers, so that each is able to see what is expected of them in the programme. In effect, the contract states what is to be done by each of the parties to make the training mission work out in practice. Contracts are signed by each of the parties, and have been found to be taken very seriously by all concerned because these signatures demonstrate the commitment they have made to the programme.

Learning contract as programme description

The contract also sets out what the programme will cover in terms of subject matter. The list is derived from the market needs analysis, and can be expected to deal with broad categories of subjects, such as leadership, communication (especially effective report-writing and presenting a case to higher management), handling people, goal-setting, managing resources, implications of employee law, and maintaining a safe working environment.

Learning contract defines rules

The contract can be the place where the programme 'rules' are made known, although these are kept to a minimum. One or two examples will show what is required. The need to achieve regular attendance is a case in point. Senior managers who nominated supervisors to the programme agreed that the period would be reserved exclusively for training. This was to avoid the disruption of supervisors being called back to work, a problem that had marred previous programmes.

Learning contract defines deadlines

Two other requirements are interesting. One was the need to set out in the contract deadlines for the return of written assignments. By signing the contract, candidates agreed to meet these deadlines. Another point which was especially important was the setting up of a mechanism to maintain effective communication about the course and its outcomes. This was to gain the candidate's agreement to produce a one-page written critique of the programme within a month of completion and discuss it in a personal interview with the senior manager.

The course critique

As well as indicating the candidate's reaction to the programme as a whole, the critique requires them to explain how closely they felt they had met their personal objectives and how they might apply their new skills to improve their working environment. The presentation of this information to the manager gave the supervisor an important way of maintaining the momentum of training. It made the manager aware that the supervisor had now gained new knowledge and skills that should be practised in the workplace. It was a logical step in the process of taking forward the training gained in the programme by giving the manager the opportunity to allow the supervisor to manage a workplace project that would further improve the way the department operated.

Too often, the end of a training programme becomes an anticlimax; the sense of achievement and confidence engendered by the programme is dissipated on return to work because there is no follow-through. Senior managers are often at fault for not taking the time to discuss what happened with course attendees, and what should be the next steps. This is a complete turn-off for trainees, as well as showing that the senior manager is not interested in checking whether there has been a return on the time and money spent on training. The point about the critique presentation is that it allows the course member to negotiate further new ways of adding value to the investment in development.

From feedback to further development

Experience gained in using this approach proves that the critique approach generates feedback between manager and course member that encourages follow-up and further development. By working through a new development in the workplace, the supervisor is able to involve employees and mould them into action learning teams that replicate the project approach learned in the supervisory development programme. The motivation of employees improves when they are expected to resolve problems and find better ways of working. In this way, the supervisor carries the benefits of the development programme forward.

The deadline for completion of the project is set into the programme timetable. It must be met, and this discipline forces effective scheduling, efficient use of time resources, and the division of labour amongst the team members so that each is seen to carry a share of the action. All these are essential components of the management task. They are learned and reinforced in the programme, and understanding of them can be transferred to employees through the example set by a supervisor.

The management of change

Action learning encourages individual self-reliance whilst enhancing a sense of partnership and synergy in the team as a whole. As they work through the project, the team encounters all the milestones that mark the continuum of classic organizational change – shock, defensive retreat, acknowledgement – leading to adaptation and change. By learning to recognize and cope with these stages in their own workplace, employees are being prepared to handle change in the wider organization and in their lives.

The supervisor also gains immeasurably when learning is reinforced after attending the development programme. Some form of follow-up mentoring will consolidate understanding of the learning process and lead to greater awareness of the interpersonal and social forces involved in managing change.

Motivation to succeed

The recommendations made by the project team to resolve the problem have to be presented to senior managers. This is motivation in itself because it gives the project team the chance to show what it can do in competition with other teams. Moreover, the work done by teams who have learned through the action learning method invariably produces a sensible attempt to recommend a course of action that will resolve, or at least ameliorate, the problem they have addressed.

CHAPTER 11

The project stage, part 3

The culmination of the action learning stage requires each of the teams to present its report and recommendations to an audience of senior managers who have commissioned the project work.

Project presentations

The presentations are an intensive and very powerful demonstration of the way supervisors will have developed over the period of the programme. Presentation sessions are the occasion when the teams can deliver an account of the work they have done to research the problem and come up with their recommendations for dealing with the issues. Many of these problems have often been unresolved before because the organization has not had the opportunity to concentrate efforts to find a solution. The structure of the supervisory management programme engineers that opportunity by using action learning as the principal means of turning teams into effective change agents.

The presentation has two main purposes. First, it gives teams the opportunity to deliver a planned exposition of the main results and recommendations reached in their study of the organizational problem. Second, it allows their presentational skills to be judged in competition with their fellow course members. Both of these objectives impose considerable pressure on the teams, which is made more stressful by the fact that the presentations are given in public and under very tight time constraints.

The panel of assessors

The presentations are also being scrutinized by a panel of assessors, who will question each team member in turn at the conclusion of their presentation to examine in depth the methodology used, and how the conclusions are supported by evidence. Assessors will report on the quality of the presentations and the projects as a whole when recommending the granting of course certificates by the accrediting body.

The assessor panel also has the responsibility to identify the team which makes the most effective presentation, and this team is awarded the Top Team trophy in an award ceremony that takes place immediately after the panel has issued its findings.

The importance of presentation skills

The concentration on presentation skills in the programme is justified by a recent survey made by Aziz Corporation, a specialist in communications strategies and techniques. The company surveyed a cross-section of directors in companies employing more than 100 staff to ascertain their views on the importance of presentation skills.

Sixty-three per cent rated presentation skills more important for success than knowing the right people (considered important by 44 per cent), intelligence (41 per cent) and financial aptitude (31 per cent). Effective presentation skills are essential tools in the locker of all managers, and training should aim to give proficiency in this field to all levels of management, starting at that of the supervisor.

Stage managing the presentations

The procedure for setting up and stage managing a presentation calls for high-order communication and project management skills on the part of the teams. They will have developed these skills whilst working on the action learning project since they are an integral function of the management of the project. Neverthe-less, teams will also need to work out in detail how they will deal with the presentation if they are to give maximum impact to the results and recommendations of the project.

The total time available for the completion of the project, including the presentation, is extremely limited. As has been noted earlier, the project stage takes place on successive Fridays over an eight-week period. This is a demanding schedule which has to cover all the preparatory work required to plan the project, identify objectives and allocate complementary roles to the indi-vidual team members.

Presentations reinforce the supervisor's role

The following account of the activities that are covered in this stage will give an insight into the range and scope of the tasks that have to be managed by the teams. It will be seen that these actions form the essence of the supervisor's role. Moreover, the project management stage provides the most comprehensive training opportunity for supervisors to develop their personal competence, and at the same time learn to appreciate the dynam-ics of team-working at first hand. If the key to supervision is the ability to pull together the skills of team members to achieve results, then the action learning stage of the supervisory develop-ment programme offers an ideal arena in which to learn how to do this.

Chronology of problem-solving

Overall, eight days (one day a week) are allocated to the teams, in which to undertake the project and resolve the problem they have been assigned.

Day 1

The morning of the first of the eight days is given over to team briefing. All the teams are assembled and given an introductory session on problem-solving, including the use of creative thinking techniques. A further session follows on action learning, with an emphasis on the application of this method to the way the project will be planned. The teams are told what facilities will be available to them at the training centre. These facilities include the allocation of trainers to act as facilitators and advisers to the teams, and the provision of training aids when the time comes to prepare materials for the presentation.

On the afternoon of this day each team begins the task of planning in detail how they will tackle the project, which is issued to them in the form of a written specification of the issue to be resolved. This specification will have been decided by a group of senior managers and is given under the authority of the chief executive of the unit concerned.

Importance of competition to motivation

This territorial ownership of the problem and its solution is important in creating the motivation to succeed amongst the teams. Each team knows that its efforts will be weighed against those of colleagues in other units of management, and they will all be aiming to bring back the Top Team trophy for their unit. Chief executives are equally enthusiastic to see their team perform well.

Days 2 to 6

During the next five Fridays, teams are free to pursue their project according to their agreed plan. In this period the team members will work to accomplish the individual tasks that have been assigned, often on their own initiative, but with the proviso that their progress has to be reported back to the team as a whole at the beginning of each Friday. This is so that every member can see how their work is contributing to the overall plan, and to decide any new initiatives that may be needed to maintain progress of the project.

Supervisors believe that the project stage is particularly valuable for their development because they are given the responsibility to handle the project management themselves. They welcome the opportunity to show their ability to work together effectively and to achieve results under pressure, knowing that they can use external facilitation whenever they need it.

In practice, this facilitation is mainly directed to helping the team members to work out their own preferred course of action to overcome a blockage that they have encountered. It is rarely necessary for the facilitator to be prescriptive unless the team is expressly unable to come to an agreement on the way to go.

The five project working days take the teams into some interesting experiences. Here they are exploring new territory, trying to discover better methods of dealing with their problem, and aiming to seek out some innovative ways that can be introduced. A good deal of their effort will be spent in questioning the present situation and the people who are involved in the issues to see what the chances of introducing change are likely to be. This is the insightful-questioning stage of action learning which can open up new avenues to explore in the search for solutions.

Seeking solutions from outside the organization

Many of the teams will extend their area of enquiry beyond the boundaries of the organization itself. They will seek out an organization from an entirely different sector where there is the prospect of learning new approaches to similar problems. This benchmarking is encouraged. Often, chief executives will be approached to act as door-openers to enable the team to visit an outside organization. In almost fifteen years there has been no occasion when an approach by a team of supervisors to visit an organization to further their knowledge and experience has been other than highly successful.

All of the data gleaned by the teams as they research the project has to be evaluated and used to construct the report. Report writing is in itself a time-consuming activity, and teams soon learn that this cannot be left to the last minute. Trainer facilitators should keep an eye on progress here to ensure that adequate time is being spent on compiling the report. The logistics of the project stage require that the report is completed by the end of the sixth Friday if time is to be available for sorting out the presentation itself.

Day 7

The seventh Friday of the total eight days allocated to the project stage is set aside for putting the presentation together and doing a dress-rehearsal. Preparing visual aids for the presentation will call for the use of skills gained in the effective presentation module held during the second week of the programme, as indicated in Chapter 5.

The presentation is a source of many good ideas for giving impact to the key points of the project and the teams need to have room to exercise their creativity. If the training venue is used as the presentation area, it should have a raised platform from which the teams will be visible. The basic presentation equipment will be an overhead projector and screen, flipcharts, a table and chairs for the team and a lectern for use by the team members in rotation as they deliver their own part of the presentation.

We have found that presentations become more sophisticated with each successive programme. Over time, incoming teams to the supervisory development programme will build on the experience of the teams that have preceded them, and it may be necessary to add other presentation aids. Early on it was found that a video recorder was required to enable a team to show a video it had made as part of its presentation. Computer-generated displays projected onto a large screen are also sometimes required.

Day 8

The final day of the project stage, seven Fridays from the initial briefing day, sees all this preparation come to a head. Five teams are able to present their findings during the morning of that day, and the total proceedings, including the assessors' verbal report to the teams and the audience and the presentation of the Top Team trophy will conclude with a buffet luncheon.

Stage management of this event must be the responsibility of trainers. It is impractical to expect teams of supervisors, all of whom are highly charged with expectation and adrenalin, to have to tend to the overall co-ordination of the morning's complex presentation programme. Supervisors will be too involved in their own affairs for that.

The order in which the teams will present their projects is determined earlier, and is most equitably arranged by drawing names out of a hat. The timetable can then be made known right at the start of the project stage. This allows the invited audience to be sent their invitations in ample time for them to block out their diaries.

Invite the major decision-makers

The sending of invitations is done by the teams themselves, but trainers will ensure that invitations go to important people in the organization, especially to the chairman and the chief executives of the various units of management.

The training programme will gain in prestige and visibility if the occasion is used to award participants with some tangible memento of the time they have spent on the programme. The most obvious of these awards is the Top Team trophy. The chairman of the authority or chief executive should present this and take the opportunity to address the course members. This ritual puts a seal of approval on the proceedings and is well appreciated by supervisors.

The team trophy does not have to be ornate. Indeed, one trophy that has been in use for many years consists of a polished block of hardwood into which a large nail is half embedded. A plaque indicates that the trophy is in recognition of the performance of the team whose name and date of award is indicated on a separate medallion affixed to the trophy. There is a fairly obvious visual pun associated with the shape and structure of this trophy. More to the point, however, is the fact that there is much competition for it, and it will be displayed in the board room of the winning unit in the period between courses with every indication of pride.

Recognize individuals

Naturally, there can only be one winner of the main trophy, but each member of the course is held to be a winner in their own right. All successful candidates will receive a certificate awarded by the Institute for Supervision and Management but, in addition, every course member is presented with a miniature replica of the wooden trophy, inscribed with their name and the dates of the course. These make good paperweights and are to be found throughout the workplaces of the organization. They provide a good talking-point and have brought the supervisors development programme to the attention of many potential candidates.

The public relations aspects of a management development programme should not be ignored. We have seen in earlier chapters that the availability of internal training has to be communicated consistently and with vigour, if only to counteract the constant flow of training advertising material that comes into the organization from outside. The presentation stage of the supervisory development programme affords an exceptional opportunity for internal and external publicity, all of which will serve to bring the programme to the attention of people who will be future participants.

Media coverage

The most effective method is to commission a local reporter and a photographer to cover the event. A presentation ceremony is a news story which will be of interest to the families and friends of candidates, as well as providing the health care organization with the chance to get some positive coverage for its policy of staff development. In the absence of press coverage, you could prepare your own news item, which should be sent to local media and to national outlets where they are available.

Because the training programme has been accredited by the ISM, the training department is able to get considerable national coverage in the pages of the ISM journal *Modern Management*, published six times a year. This publication has earned an enviable reputation for its breadth of coverage of management topics and is valuable to public service trainers and managers for the insights it gives into other sectors. Much of the publicity our training strategy gained in its pages was instrumental in bringing the supervisory development programme to the attention of health care organizations across the UK.

Internal publicity should also be promoted through the organization's official staff journal, if one is published. If not, the training department should produce its own training newsletter, and make a commitment to publishing it regularly. A quarterly publication is adequate, and should have a prime target readership amongst influential managers in the organization as well as those supervisors and middle managers who constitute the main training and development client base.

Build on the work of teams

In a sense, a development programme is never fully completed. The work of the teams will be perpetuated in the project reports, and a copy of these will be retained in the training library, where they will provide a source of study for future course members. Some projects may be taken up by future teams for the purpose of building on the work that has been done and creating an improved version of the original result. This is an example of internal benchmarking – using a prototype as the basis to build a better, Mark 2, version.

The next logical step in the development of the supervisors who have worked to recommend a solution to an operational problem is to empower them to implement solutions that show particular promise. To bring about a better way of doing things is the acid test of innovation. Unless senior managers are willing to sponsor innovation, they will damage the motivation of project teams and fail to realize the ultimate benefits that the action learning approach can bring to the development of people and the organization.

Where senior managers do give action learning teams the chance to test their recommended plan, then significant cultural and operational changes occur. Empowering the supervisor to manage the implementation of the plan is a signal that top management takes the exercise seriously and is interested in seeing how the proposed plan will turn out.

Test the solutions

This message will be even stronger if senior managers commission each team to try their ideas out in the form of a prototype. Senior managers know all too well that snags will arise in the implementation stage, but they cannot expect their protégés to realize learning benefits unless they are allowed to take some risks.

People need to be permitted to fail, and one consequence of this approach is that failures can be contained within the prototype stage without impinging too seriously on the mainstream operation.

The prototype approach to implementing the changes recommended by project teams should become a logical follow-on from the development programme itself. In effect, the learning process is only partly completed if recommendations are not put to the test and the intended results assessed. This means that the learning objectives of the programme can only be fully realized by making the implementation of the project a mandatory requirement.

This requires the co-operation of managers, especially those in whose area of responsibility the prototype will be tested. They will be required to oversee the development and may need to reallocate resources to achieve the planned results. On the other hand, they have the longer-term prospect of seeing beneficial changes being introduced through the efforts of their own employees, with a consequent improvement in morale and performance.

Monitoring progress

A project taken forward for implementation should be recorded by the training department to allow them to monitor progress against agreed milestones. This mechanism also allows the trainer to continue to engage the project team in discussions about their continuing personal development after they leave the programme.

It is an important means of retaining interest in continuous development.

There is an added advantage in the trainer being involved with a prototype development – it gives the opportunity to create a training centre in the workplace in partnership with the supervisor. Having experienced the action learning process, the supervisor will know that it can play an important role in the development of employees.

The training department can capitalize on this by offering to help the supervisor establish an action learning group in the workplace. This leaves the supervisor free to concentrate on the logistics and management of the workplace project, whilst the trainer briefs employees on the basics of action learning, acts as the team facilitator, and helps participants to realize their learning objectives. In this way, it is possible to extend the benefits of training beyond the boundaries of the management development programme.

Word of mouth will soon spread the message that the organization is supporting the development of its managers as it commissions them to deal with real problems in creative and innovative ways. This approach will lead to a deeper understanding of how attitudes and behaviour can be changed by using the power of action learning more widely in the organization. Supervisors become the vanguard for introducing into the workplace the techniques of change-making they have studied and learned in the laboratory conditions of their development programme.

In this chapter, we have given an in-depth view of the dynamics that animate an action learning programme designed to be a development tool for supervisors. The team approach to change-making requires supervisors to study and learn a number of skills. They do this as they work together to achieve the goals of the project. Learning is a natural outcome of the search for solutions and becomes an essential part of their personal development.

But the acquisition of these skills provides them with much more than the ability to gain a qualification. The skills become an integral part of their management toolkit, to be used and reused in their day-to-day management. These are skills that foster the capacity to confront problems rather than ignore them. Project-based learning makes self-reliant managers.

CHAPTER 12

Evaluation

Evaluating whether training results in organizational effectiveness has always been difficult, but some measures are needed to establish whether the resources put into training are making a contribution that at least offsets the cost.

It is often possible to attribute monetary values to the benefits achieved, especially in the areas of performance, such as improved job productivity, that can be measured against predetermined criteria. In the supervisory development programme, this type of evaluation can be developed and carried out as a partnership activity between the manager who authorizes the training and the supervisor who undertakes it.

Both the sponsor and the supervisor need to have a clear appreciation of the level of knowledge and skills and the personal attributes that the supervisor has to command in order to carry out the role effectively. They need to agree how the supervisor currently performs before undertaking any training. This review gives a profile of the incumbent's present competence, and can be used to identify existing training and development needs. The profile will be compared after the training has been completed with a new, different profile, and so will identify changes that can be attributed to the supervisor having been on the programme.

Assessing performance

There are three steps to assessing job performance:

1 The sponsor and the supervisor separately identify the competence profile of the supervisor, as each perceives it.
2 The sponsor and the supervisor separately formulate a profile of how they consider an 'ideal' supervisor would carry out the role if performing at optimum capacity.
3 The sponsor and the supervisor jointly compare these profiles and identify the gaps that exist between actual and optimum performance.

This method has several advantages. It involves the manager and the supervisor in drawing up the subordinate role specification, and allows each to explore fully their personal perceptions of the job. Since these understandings can differ widely, some mechanism is required to allow each person to clarify what needs to be done so that they can mutually agree the content of the supervisor's role and affirm the priority to be given to aspects of the job.

Step 1: Define present performance specification

Step 1 works by allowing the manager and supervisor to construct two separate specifications of the supervisor's role as seen from their own perspectives. It is rare for these viewpoints to be the same because managers do not necessarily share with their supervisors the same set of expectations of the way the job ought to be carried out. Each has to see the job through his or her own eyes in order to begin to bring these views into harmony and form an agreed picture of the intricacies of the job. Unless this step is taken at the outset, there is a danger that either the manager or the supervisor, or both, will be dissatisfied with the ultimate performance, because neither was completely in agreement with what had to be achieved.

These differences are brought out in the subsequent discussion between the manager and the supervisor. The aim is for both parties to agree an acceptable role specification that will be realistic and realizable. Much of the difficulty of improving personal performance is due to manager and subordinate operating to different blueprints of what the job should be. Where one believes there is room for improvement in one dimension, the other is likely to feel performance is satisfactory. Mutual understanding of the standards of competence required in the job are needed before any serious assessment can be made to identify the skills which need to be developed if the supervisor is to meet expected levels of performance.

It is not uncommon for managers who sit down with their supervisors to clarify a role to be astonished to find that their individual perceptions of the job differ so much. They are then faced with the choice of begging to differ, and so perpetuating the confusion, or coming to an agreement on the job requirements.

The sensible approach is to negotiate an optimum role specification that they both feel is appropriate in the circumstances. This not only results in greater mutual understanding of the job requirements, but also begins to build a better working relationship between them. These positions will be further consolidated as the supervisor works through the development programme to fill the gaps in competence that have been uncovered, and the manager becomes involved in the mentoring role.

Step 2: Define optimum desired performance specification

Step 2 builds a picture of what the role could be. A practical way of doing this is to use the Management Charter Initiative (MCI) standards that describe the supervisory role and employ these as the benchmark for identifying the basic competences required for effective performance in the job.

The competences describe the recognized specifications and standards of performance expected of managers. Using them to compile a picture of what a capable supervisor should do makes sense because the list is comprehensive and embraces all aspects of the management role as applied to UK organizations. Some organizations, amongst them the NHS, have translated the MCI competences to make them more easily understood in the prevailing cultural idiom, but this has not altered the basis of the management role which they describe.

Step 3: Define what development is needed for optimum performance

Step 3 of the process for assessing job performance requires a joint meeting between the manager and the supervisor. Here, they together identify the areas where current actual performance differs from the optimum performance derived from their study of the MCI standards. This meeting will enable both parties to gain greater awareness of where coaching or training is necessary to help the supervisor meet the standards.

The three steps of the competence review exercise not only clearly define what is expected from the supervisor, but give the manager important clues as to where support should be given, either on-the-job with the manager acting as a coach, or off-the-job in the supervisory development programme. By feeding details of the training needs to the trainer, sponsoring managers help trainers to design a programme that meets real and specific needs.

There is an added advantage in discovering the supervisor's training needs by this method. The process of joint discussion between the supervisor and the manager is a valuable opportunity for them both to concentrate on the aspects of performance that need to be given attention. They will be able to agree an order of priority for tackling the needs, and so begin to formulate a personal development plan for the supervisor to follow under the guidance of the manager.

The closer manager and supervisor can join together in a partnership of learning, the greater the ultimate benefits can be. The manager will be assured that specific issues of under-performance have been identified, and that these will be remedied in the development programme. The supervisor will be confident that the method of identifying shortcomings in performance has been relatively objective, involving the crucial element of self-appraisal against nationally recognized standards of competence. Being involved in identifying what needs to be improved gives the supervisor greater ownership of the subsequent development plan.

Benefits for the trainer

Finally, the trainer will discover the authentic problems of under-performance in the client group. This ensures that the training to be offered is grounded in the real world. Moreover, the trainer can use this method of assessing performance against standards of competence to build up the tripartite partnership between the sponsoring manager, the supervisor and the training function. These are the principal players in the search for improved performance, and their close involvement is critical to the ultimate success of the development programme.

Evaluating performance with Management Charter Initiative standards

Each training syllabus will be different because they reflect the changing needs of a particular cross-section of supervisors, but a trainer looking for a useful categorization of topics of importance in supervisory management development will find that the most valuable research has been carried out already under the auspices of the Management Charter Initiative.

MCI is the operating arm of the National Forum for Management Education and Development, with a mission to promote management development, and particularly competence-based development, for the benefit of both organizations and individuals. It is the main source of information on the nationally agreed occupational standards applicable to managers at all levels.

These standards define the competences expected of managers carrying out their range of tasks, and provide yardsticks known as National Vocational Qualifications (NVQs) by which to measure competent performance. They are available for virtually all occupations in the UK and, since they have been adapted to apply to managers in the NHS, will give management developers in the health care sector a framework for designing relevant training based on the most rigorous assessment of what makes an effective manager.

The management vocational qualifications are graded into levels according to a manager's degree of authority and range of activities. Management level 3 and management level 4 contain the essential competences needed by supervisors and first-line managers, and a development programme based on these will meet the needs of the majority of managers catered for in the programme described here.

However, there are some operational and strategic activities described in management level 5 which may be incorporated into the job descriptions of some junior managers. For example, some of the candidates put forward for entry to the supervisory development programme may have a responsibility to pro-actively identify and implement change (a strategic activity at level 5), whereas levels 3 and 4 need only a more limited contribution to be made in this area.

MCI standards and the trainer

The main use of the MCI standards is to enable the trainer to mix and match the competences required to ensure the programme contains learning opportunities that will stretch those under training and give them a grounding in the practice of measuring their own competence against nationally agreed standards.

The standards are an essential part of any self-directed personal development programme and are important because they allow the manager to see the gap between present and optimum performance. This perception is essential if the manager is to decide whether improvement has to be made, and then to decide what to do about it.

The reference to MCI standards does not imply that a supervisory development programme has to be directed to the attainment of National Vocational Qualifications. NVQs will provide a valuable outcome for successful candidates and are sought after in organizations (like the NHS) that value certification. But there is some merit in avoiding clouding the set-up of a new supervisory prototype development programme by introducing NVQs too soon.

Why is this? One reason is that the NVQ system has to be administered through a relatively complex and somewhat bureaucratic infrastructure of internal and external assessors. There is also an element of additional cost, which will have to be met out of the programme start-up budget. Trying to introduce a prototype development programme and at the same time run a new NVQ system may prove difficult, and it is preferable to concentrate all available energy into making a success of the training before seeking to have it accredited.

It is relatively easy to overlay in-house management development programmes with the accreditation criteria laid down by an appropriate professional body at a later stage, and then to judge whether they meet the criteria and can therefore be approved by the awarding body. This is a worthwhile way of adding value to what is being done in the organization to develop managers. Advice on how this can be achieved is available from the Institute for Supervision and Management or from other similar sources (see the list of useful addresses on pages 179–82).

The assessment method provides more than a list of gaps in performance. The MCI competences define what the supervisor has to be capable of doing and describe the criteria against which effective performance can be judged. Knowledge of these performance standards is extremely useful for managers. By studying them, it is possible to build up a picture of the actions an effective manager takes to carry out a specific part of the role.

Visualizing is one of the key representation systems used in our western culture. Through it, we are able to 'see' in our mind's eye who and what we would like to be, and form images of the steps we need to take to arrive at that perception. Through the medium of the performance criteria, the manager can visualize the steps to be taken to reach a desired standard of performance. The clearer the manager can perceive the desired end-state, as set out in the performance criteria, the more likely it is that appropriate steps can be formulated to achieve it.

Key roles of managers

The MCI standards are made up of seven units, each of which categorizes a key role of management. Taken together, the seven units form an integrated structure describing the work of a manager (see Figure 12.1).

Key role A: Manage activities   Key role E: Manage energy
Key role B: Manage resources   Key role F: Manage quality
Key role C: Manage people   Key role G: Manage projects
Key role D: Manage information

Figure 12.1   The seven Key roles

Here is an example of how a study of the standards can assist a supervisor to take action to remedy a workplace problem. Take the case of a supervisor who has identified that there is a need to minimize conflict in the team. Using the self-assessment method described above, the first step is to look up the MCI standards and decide which key role addresses the issue of team conflict. Obviously, this comes into the area of managing people, Key role C. This describes the work of managers in getting the most from their teams. The description goes on to list seventeen essential elements of the managerial role that are used in managing people. From this list one element, Unit C5 *Develop productive working relationships*, seems to describe an appropriate goal for the supervisor to work towards.

The next step is to look further into Unit C5. It will be found to be divided into the following elements:

C5.1 Develop the trust and support of colleagues and team members.
C5.2 Develop the trust and support of your manager.
C5.3 Minimize interpersonal conflict.

The supervisor can now decide which of these elements, or indeed what combination of them, need to be worked on to minimize the problem of interpersonal conflict. A start can then be made to find the best practice to employ. Seeking advice from the trainer, an appropriate training event can be found and a decision made to gain some knowledge that can be used to overcome the interpersonal issues at the root of the main problem. The main point is that something is being done to rectify the situation.

There are a number of performance criteria which show appropriate actions that can be taken to deal with performance failures across the full spectrum of supervisory management activities. From these, it is possible to select those that the supervisor feels are appropriate to use in the circumstances. Subsequent action taken in accordance with the standard criteria will give the supervisor a learning opportunity to see whether the results are effective in changing the situation.

In the case we are discussing, the supervisor will act to fulfil one or more of the criteria listed above in C5.1, C5.2, or C5.3. In doing so, proven methods are taken for dealing with the problem of conflict in the team. Action based on the performance criteria might include, for example:

- providing opportunities for individuals to discuss problems which directly or indirectly affect their work (criterion b);
- taking action promptly to deal with conflicts between individuals (criterion c);
- making recommendations promptly to the relevant people for improving procedures and reducing the potential for conflict (criterion h).

Remedying poor performance by self-help

One advantage of using the MCI standards is that the manager is given a tool with which to break down a management problem into a set of remedial actions. This opens up real opportunities for personal development by enabling the manager to visualize the actions needed to respond to problems, and then to move from visualizing what needs to be done to actually doing something constructive that is in accordance with accepted standards of managerial performance.

Not all organizations use the MCI standards to evaluate the competence of their managers and supervisors. The reasons for this are varied. Some schools of thought hold that too much bureaucracy and red tape surround the whole of the drive towards establishing national qualifications. A contrary view holds that the process is expensive to administer in terms of management time and energy. Supporters of the system counter this argument with the view that the expenses of education can be calculated, and budgets can be set aside to broaden the competence of people. The cost of ignorance, on the other hand, is incalculable.

Competitive advantage through people

Increasingly, it is being recognized that organizations can only gain lasting competitive advantage by releasing the potential of their people. People represent a sustainable resource whose capacity can be continually renewed if opportunities are provided and methods introduced to promote and foster self-development by everyone in the organization. So far, we have discussed how an individual manager's management training and development needs can be identified by comparing present performance against some preferred future state. This provides the goals to work towards by clearly specifying how the individual will be able to act in carrying out the managerial role. The effectiveness of that plan can only be realized fully by following a planned schedule of active learning, designed to improve the application of new skills, and apply them in practice.

Evaluation by defining financial benefits

The effectiveness of the supervisory programme can be evaluated by assessing the financial benefits that the organization gains by having real and pressing problems solved. Quantifying the team's efforts in this way will appeal to senior managers, who are more used to judging results in cost–benefit terms.

This approach to training evaluation can and should be planned into the projects from the beginning. In order to give objectivity to the cost-recording procedure, trainers will do well to involve their colleagues from the finance function in drawing up a methodology for costing all the inputs to the project and all the quantifiable outputs so that these can be compared in financial terms.

Here is an example of what is needed. In the model programme, we have seen that each separate project researched in the project stage of the development programme will take the time and energy resources of four supervisors, working as a team. They are commissioned to research, analyse, make recommendations and present a report to resolve an operational problem. This is essentially the culmination of the learning they have achieved together in the initial stages of their development programme, and is the vehicle for testing their ability to plan how they might put their learning into practical effect.

They are allocated six days to complete the project, so the cost of their time is easily calculated as the product of their collective earnings over the six-day period.

The lost opportunity cost, represented by paying for alternative cover for the time they will be away from their workplace, may also be added. However, staffing levels are rarely sufficient to compensate for supervisors attending courses, and the experience of running this kind of development programme in the NHS is that no official cover can be provided.

The costs of other inputs include the following:

- research (books, journal cuttings, Internet sources);
- travel (many teams who are allowed to visit other organizations for benchmarking purposes report on the value of broadening their horizons in this way);
- clerical support (typing, photocopying, binding completed reports, producing visual aids for the project);
- the total cost of the training function input (staffing, training materials, venue costs, etc. can be allocated to the project stage, on a pro rata basis if necessary).

The intention is to arrive at a figure that accounts for the cost of the time and resources spent by the team in undertaking the work needed to resolve the set problem. These are the costs of the inputs.

Added value

The value of the outcomes is more difficult to assess, but a notional value can be attributed to indicate the added value that would accrue if the solutions recommended by the project team were to be implemented. Although this consequential value of the solution cannot be accurately gauged until the solution has been implemented, a fair estimate should be made so that the feasibility of testing the solution can be considered. This will help to decide whether the project recommendations should be introduced to provide tangible evidence of the actual benefits of the new approach. Even where a full-scale application is not felt to be desirable at that time, the notional cost savings can be compared with the input costs incurred by the team and an estimate of value reached.

It is a worthwhile exercise to insist that this cost–benefit analysis is done by independent audit. This will give more weight to the findings and underline the management message that, wherever possible, training should be subjected to financial scrutiny to establish whether the benefits outweigh the costs incurred in doing it.

The values arising from personal and team development that are listed above can be measured with a greater degree of precision than some of the other benefits that accrue from training. This point can be illustrated by considering how to gauge the value of the soft skills acquired by individuals in the teamworking phase of the management development programme, which are notoriously difficult to quantify in comparison to the evaluation of hard skills.

Hard skills

Team problem-solving is highly effective in developing the hard skills, like strategic planning, goal-setting, resource allocation, organizing, decision-making and applying sound judgement, that are needed to find a solution to the problem. Reaching a satisfactory end-result by solving the problem confirms that the team has displayed these hard skills in getting to the goal. But there is increasing awareness that transformational leaders need to balance their hard-skill abilities by the judicious use of the so-called soft skills that many observers believe are needed in the work culture of today.

Soft skills

Transformational leaders require soft-skill characteristics such as vision, charisma, the ability to set an example that will inspire others, and to get the best from all resources, especially people.

Good interpersonal attributes figure largely in the armoury of these leaders. They are surprisingly absent from many public-service managers, who continue to adopt authoritarian attitudes to manage their people with little awareness that employees expect to be treated differently.

The new generation coming onto the job market will be more likely to respond to the participative style of management that treats people as partners in seeking organizational survival and growth by working together in a joint venture. Managing people by edict is becoming outmoded, and training and development should aim to enhance soft-skill abilities.

Quality of working life

Some pointers to why managers need to improve their ability to generate a better quality of life at work is emerging from research in the US and UK. This is suggesting that there is a strong link between modern people-management and organizational performance. For example, the Institute of Work Psychology has reported that job satisfaction accounts for as much as 25 per cent of the variation in productivity between organizations. This is an extremely high factor when compared with the difference in productivity attributed to research and development (6 per cent), competitive strategy (less than 3 per cent), and technology (1 per cent). Yet the underlying reasons for this variance are not understood by all managers, and many continue to concentrate on learning more about the strategic issues of business than about the techniques they need to help people to contribute more effectively in line with the mission and aims of their organization.

There is a challenge here for organizations to rethink their approach to developing people. A starting-point can be found by reforming the way supervisors are developed so that they can in turn develop their teams. In the light of the Institute of Work Psychology study, this may require management development to concentrate more on providing supervisors with the soft skills and techniques they need to be able to motivate their teams to excellent performance above and beyond present levels.

Supervisors who have learned these skills, by actually practising them in team projects, have reported in their end-of-programme debriefings that they have heightened their awareness of what motivates them at work. This knowledge has opened their eyes to how they can transfer this insight into ways of managing their own teams when they return to work.

Developing 'people skills'

Much of the true value of the team project stage of the development programme comes from the improvement of the supervisor's soft skills. In the project, supervisors learn how to handle individuals and teams, to be better communicators, and to find effective ways to help their team achieve goals. Above all, supervisors have consistently reported that they have heightened their knowledge of the human dimension and increased their skill in handling people during this stage. The ability to apply this knowledge and skill is one of the most valuable outcomes of their training.

Evaluation of development is essential if evidence is to be collected to see that it is meeting the planned objectives. Pre-planned outcomes express what the end-product of the training will be, and give a yardstick for measuring success or otherwise in achieving the desired results.

Self-assessment

Evaluation can be carried out by an individual manager using the self-assessment technique to compare present competence against a desired future state of competence. This can be based on the competences set out in the Management Charter Initiative, or by using competences established within the organization.

Joint assessment

It is desirable to involve the senior manager in a joint assessment of the competences required in a role, since the exercise gives the two parties greater understanding of the gaps in knowledge, skill, and behaviour that are impeding present performance. Joint assessment also engages the senior manager more closely in the learning process, and gives the opportunity for the senior to become a mentor.

Cost the effectiveness of the project

The problem-solving project can be evaluated objectively by designing a cost analysis into it to attempt to quantify the benefits of introducing the recommendations made by the project team. Teams of supervisors who are commissioned to resolve problems that come within their operational orbit will invariably show an intense motivation to succeed. This will lead them to exhibit a very strong desire to bring about a resolution of the problem. Consequently, it is highly probable that the outcome of this type of action learning activity will be a solution that will show significant benefits to the organization. It should be implemented if circumstances permit and further evaluation made to measure the contribution that better management has made to organizational performance.

Personal and organizational development combined

Action learning projects provide organizations with the means to achieve two mutually supportive outcomes. First, managers are developed in the skills of their profession in a constructive and practical way that draws on their capacity to learn from their own experience. Second, the organization overcomes a real operational barrier by having it tackled by a motivated management taskforce.

There is enormous potential within the ranks of supervisory management waiting to be released through effective training. The justification for evaluating training will be provided by the evidence that this contention is true.

CHAPTER 13

Recognition

People need to be praised

It is normal for human beings to seek the recognition of their peers, yet it is a paradox that organizations regularly fail to give recognition to employees for effective performance even when the opportunity occurs. Managers often perpetuate a culture of non-recognition because their own good performance is not acknowledged, except perhaps in an off-hand way. Yet the benefits to morale, commitment and general well-being of managers and employees alike can be significantly improved by giving some form of praise where praise is due.

When occasions arise for offering recognition, they should not be ignored, but treated appropriately and consistently so that the recognition behaviour becomes as normal a response as its counterpart, the rebuke. A working atmosphere where praising and rebuking people is kept in some sort of balance shows the manager is even-handed. This perception will be reciprocated by a general improvement in team spirit, especially where employees believe their worth has not been acknowledged in the past.

Recognizing learning

It is also important to recognize good performance in the management development programme, and trainers should make a practice of consciously looking for evidence that learning goals are being achieved by candidates and acknowledging their progress. Most candidates find the transition from the workplace to the training room somewhat daunting. Often they are unsure of their ability to absorb new learning, or may lack confidence that they can keep up with their colleagues. These are natural reactions to their new situation, but a well-timed word of encouragement will do much to counteract any feelings of inadequacy.

Praising

When the need to praise arises, it brings up the question of whether to praise in private or in public. Unlike giving rebukes, which are as a rule more effective where the individual is taken aside from the team and dealt with out of earshot, praising people works the other way. Giving praise is a public endorsement that progress has been made by an individual.

Positive benefits of recognition

By giving praise in public, two complementary benefits are achieved. First, the individual is justly commended and gains recognition of this fact from the peer group. Second, the group gets a vicarious pleasure in seeing one of their number receive recognition for progress made. An astute trainer can turn this situation into a useful learning opportunity for all.

The trainer can point out that, whereas general progress has been made by the course members as a whole, the purpose of referring to an individual's progress is to compensate for the fact that praise is so seldom given for good performance in the workplace. In subsequent group discussion on this point, it is almost invariably agreed that supervisors are not good at receiving or giving praise. Many state that they rarely get praise from their own managers when they achieve first-class performance, so are therefore not inclined to recognize the achievements of their employees in this way.

Negative attitudes to recognition

Unwillingness on the part of managers and supervisors to praise and show respect for good performance is an all too common reaction in organizations. A start can be made in the training room to change this behaviour by showing that deserved praise can and should be given to employees. There is a lesson here that can be easily learned if the occasion is used to help candidates reflect on the feelings they get after receiving praise for their performance on the development programme. They can then be encouraged to consider the likelihood that their own team members will also share these same feelings of improved confidence and self-esteem if they are treated in a similar way. This insight has been known to have a profound effect on the subsequent behaviour of supervisors, entirely disproportionate to the simplicity of the lesson itself.

The rule in praising is the reverse of that for rebuking. Rebuking starts with finding someone doing things wrong. Praising begins by finding someone doing things right, and then taking action to acknowledge that correct experience so as to reinforce the behaviour that led to it.

Public recognition

Just as people benefit from having their performance recognized, so a management development programme should aim to gain public recognition for developing its clients to acceptable standards. The highest standard of achievement for training is found in the National Training Awards. All trainers responsible for the development of training programmes should make it a point to become fully conversant with the purpose and procedures of these awards.

The scheme was set up in 1987 to encourage and reward exceptional training in the UK. It is an important contribution to the training and development of employees because it highlights the relationship between investment in training and development and improved business performance. By underlining this central issue, the award helps the trainer to focus on the core strategic purpose of the training function, that of maximizing business performance through people.

National Training Awards

The National Training Award proved to be an important goal for the trainers who designed the management development programme for supervisors and middle managers in one NHS health authority. It was seen from the outset that management development needed to be modelled on the best standards available. The National Training Award provided an accepted national yardstick to measure the key components of the programme, and enabled the training team to concentrate on designing training to a specification that had national endorsement.

Aiming high

To gain high standards it is necessary to aim for them, and the decision to test the in-house programme in the national arena proved to be an exceptionally demanding discipline as well as an intense learning opportunity for the training team. In 1988, one year after the inception of the scheme, the health authority became the first to win a National Training Award for a supervisory management development programme delivered in-house. This achievement, against a field of 1500 competitors, fully vindicated the decision to explore an entirely new approach to developing supervisors and managers within the organization.

The health care organization achieved this award at a time of extreme organizational change, when many believed that efforts should be directed to consolidation rather than to innovation. But the training team took the view that the implementation of a radical new development should be tested against organizations competing for the National Training Awards. Although an element of healthy competition is a motivating factor, the main impetus to entering the award scheme was to test the development programme in the marketplace and receive feedback from the scheme's examiners. Of course, the winning of an award is important, but it is the knowledge that the quality of the training programme has been recognized at the highest level that counts.

The opportunity to test a training programme in this way may not be available to all trainers, but it is important for them to actively look for methods to compare their in-house programmes and training strategies against those in other organizations. One of the criticisms levelled against in-house programmes is that they can become too inward looking because they lack contact with external developments.

Benchmark training and development

There may be some justification in this, but the remedy is for the trainer to establish a network of contacts amongst fellow trainers in other organizations and, indeed, in other sectors of industry, commerce and public services. Regular sharing of experiences and insights about training and development between different organizations can do much to bring new ideas to bear on the development of managers, and overcome insular thinking.

Recognizing the individual

Important as national recognition is to an organization, the same principles of public acknowledgement for candidates who complete management development programmes can easily be replicated in in-house training procedures, and will have similar results in motivating and rewarding candidates.

Reward systems in training work best when each member of the development programme receives a personal endorsement of achievement. That is why it is so important to have in-house training programmes endorsed by an external professional organization that can award an appropriate certificate or diploma to candidates. We have seen that the presentation of these qualifications by the chairman or chief executive, at a properly stage-managed ceremony, can be a highly acceptable way of publicly recognizing the performance of course members. Making this occasion the opportunity for further publicity, by inviting the local press and photographer to cover the event in the media, will provide the organization with good public relations. Photographs of course members can also be displayed at the training venue as a permanent record of progress, as well as being provided as personal mementoes.

Internal publicity and advertising

In addition, the coverage of project presentations should feature in organizational newsletters to promote internal training and attract candidates for future programmes. The almost universal availability of desktop publishing enables most training departments to compile their own newsletter to publicize presentation ceremonies. This is a valuable form of marketing for training, which we have seen carried out to good effect in the team project stage.

Even more valuable is the word-of-mouth advertising that comes from discussions that successful candidates have with their colleagues after the programme. The trainer can use this to good advantage by arranging for groups of potential candidates to be addressed by two or three previous course members at information sessions held before recruiting begins for future courses. These sessions are useful for showing the positive advantages of the development programme, as well as allowing many minor concerns to be cleared up.

Keeping on side with colleagues

A large part of the success of in-house training and development programmes can be attributed to the close co-operation that trainers have been able to generate with managers at all levels. Their understanding and active involvement are essential in helping to specify the programme content, to assist as mentors and lecturers, and assess the standards of competence reached by course members. This sets a pattern for future co-operation between trainers and line managers that is able to see the manager's role as workplace trainer and assessor extend into the field of National Vocational Qualifications, together with a substantially increased participation of senior managers as course tutors.

Recognizing success through National Vocational Qualifications

Organizations adopting National Vocational Qualifications to measure and improve the ability of their employees understand the value of developing their supervisors to become workplace trainers. Even if the organization prefers to base training on its own standards of competence instead of endorsing national competences, the importance of having effective supervisors to manage learning cannot be overestimated. The project stage of the supervisory development programme will identify those supervisors who can be given further training to become an increasingly extensive group of workplace trainers throughout the organization.

CHAPTER 14

External partnerships

It was shown in earlier chapters that alliances formed by trainers within their organization are valuable in providing successful training. Training has to sell itself on the benefits it will bring to people and organizations. By casting the net widely over prospective clients, it is possible to contact those who need to know that there is training available which can offer them the prospect of personal advancement. Trainers who build up co-operative partnerships by networking with their colleagues at all levels are spreading the message that training can help them to achieve more.

As well as cultivating partnerships within the organization, trainers also need to be resolute about extending their networks into the outside world. There is a proliferation of links that can be made. The most beneficial are the networks made with the many agencies that have been set up to facilitate the application of government initiatives, especially those that focus on human resource issues.

Government support for training and development

In the UK, the government is a prime supporter of training and development targeted to the field of economic development, and especially to that aspect of development that comes from the effective utilization of people. The responsibility is to ensure that the quality and quantity of human resources available can meet the challenges of competitors on anything like equal terms. This imperative has its roots in the unpalatable fact that in many fields the nation does not meet world-class standards.

The principal government departments that channel support for training are the Department for Education and Employment and the Department of Trade and Industry. Regional assemblies in Scotland and Wales will also play an extensive part to ensure that national training initiatives are successfully deployed and get the results required.

Local agencies

Trainers in public and private sectors, by the nature of their work, will be familiar with the role and responsibilities of the agencies that implement central government measures locally. The most visible of these agencies are the Training and Enterprise Councils of England and Wales. (TECs). Together with their counterparts, Local Enterprise Companies in Scotland (LECs) and the Training and Employment Agency for Northern Ireland, they have a major responsibility to manage government funded schemes.

TECs have been established to provide a partnership with employers and others concerned with the regeneration of economic activity within regions. It is therefore especially important that trainers acting on behalf of their employing organization seek every opportunity to work in partnership with TECs to gain mutual advantages.

TECs and LECs deliver youth and adult training programmes to meet the labour market requirements of the locality. They do this by contracting with national and local training providers for the supply of appropriate training courses, materials and services. It is obvious that there is an opportunity here for trainers in organizations to pool resources with TECs, and so help to tackle problems such as lack of skills in the labour market.

Networking and collaborative partnerships

The trainer within an organization can be extremely influential by acting as a link to create an active partnership between the organization and local agencies. The trainer has to be opportunistic and entrepreneurial in approach. Opportunism is displayed by actively seeking out the agency officers who deal with government schemes and building up a rapport with them. Discussions will uncover the areas where joint working is likely to bear fruit. Having identified these, the trainer has to show entrepreneurialism by working on a plan to bring the partnership into existence.

In this chapter, we will consider how joint collaboration was achieved between the NHS health care organization that developed the supervisory training model detailed in this book and its local TEC. This example of a collaborative partnership shows the advantages of this approach, which resulted in the training function being able both to increase its own training capacity and to add to the organization's recruitment and retention capability.

This case study provides useful guidance to trainers seeking to set up a partnership arrangement with an outside agency. The main lesson we learned was that trainers could improve the performance of their role by working in partnership with an outside agency to help achieve mutual goals. Numerous opportunities to set up similar partnership agreements can be found by those who take time and effort to study the reports and plans of government agencies. The annual reports of TECs, for instance, show the progress made on a range of initiatives, and give valuable pointers to future projects that will have an impact on the employment and training strategies of employers in their area.

Finding openings

TEC reports should be mandatory reading for trainers who will need the intelligence they provide to identify where joint working would lead to mutual advantage. This gives leads that can be followed through with enthusiasm and tenacity. Collaborative working arrangements of this kind are major opportunities for learning, as well as avenues to significant benefits for the organization.

Whilst this case deals with a collaborative networking developed by trainers, the principles and practice of networking and co-operative joint working are also available to line managers. Many partnership projects exist in the public service, for example, between NHS Trusts and the social service departments of local government, with voluntary agencies in the health care field, and in research projects with universities. These are normally initiated by senior managers, however, and it is strongly suggested that opportunities for setting up joint collaborative projects with the external organizations should be made available to supervisors.

The main point here is that there are many opportunities available for joint working and co-operative partnerships with other agencies. By their nature, collaborative ventures provide rich learning opportunities for all concerned, and managers who value personal and professional development will gain significantly in expertise and influence by acting decisively to recognize and seize these opportunities.

Supervisors should be required to consider how their own functions might benefit from adopting a networking approach with a partner organization or agency, and be given the responsibility to develop effective joint working arrangements on the lines indicated below.

An external partnership in action

Our example of joint partnership is based on Employment Training (ET), a programme that was set up to give unemployed people, particularly the long-term unemployed, the skills and experience they would need in order to get and keep jobs. Our study relates specifically to the initiatives taken by trainers to establish their employer as a provider of Employment Training at the beginning of this national initiative. Since then, ET has been superseded by new initiatives, such as the New Deal measures, and this trend will no doubt be followed by further variations on the theme of helping people to deal with unemployment. The fact that a system changes, however, does not invalidate the principle that it is more productive to find ways of working together than to try to work alone.

When Employment Training was introduced in September 1988, the health authority in question was already three years into operating its supervisory development programme. This had by then been extended beyond its original conception of a team-based problem-solving approach, and different ways of developing two different management groups were being demanded.

Coping with increased demand for training

One of these groups comprised a growing population of employees who were aspiring to get a foot on the supervisory management career ladder. The second group consisted of more senior supervisors (many of whom had completed the original development programme), together with an increasing number of middle managers who were actively looking to improve their performance and career opportunities. Whilst this showed a high regard for the quality of in-house training, it gave the training function a seemingly insurmountable barrier to overcome if it was to extend the scale of training and development to these clients.

The barrier was lack of funding. The remedy was to see whether the training department could itself generate the income it needed to develop its activities. This line of thinking led inevitably to the idea of establishing an alliance with a partner organization that was similarly committed to extending training through a range of training providers.

Opening the dialogue

The obvious step was to develop a dialogue with the agency responsible for introducing Employment Training to the area. So networking with the Training Agency and its successor the local Training and Enterprise Council began, which was to be of substantial benefit to the two organizations, and to the unemployed.

The idea was floated informally in discussions with the chief executives of both organizations, and their interest and tacit approval allowed more detailed discussions to be opened up with influential senior decision-makers in the two organizations, in particular with the directorates of planning and finance. Many other senior health care managers were lobbied, especially those in the operational areas of nursing and administration where employment trainees would be deployed for training and work experience.

Discussion groups were also set up with trade union officials to try to overcome the 'political' problems they perceived were embedded into the ET scheme. There was considerable opposition at that time to the requirement that employment trainees should be accepted onto the scheme on a 'benefit plus' basis, that is, they received a bonus of £10 per week over and above the level of their normal social benefit. This negative response had to be debated and overcome if the joint project was to proceed with any prospect of success.

Building the business case

Whilst these discussions were in progress, the business case for the proposed arrangements was being prepared. Essentially, this dealt with the logistics and management of the scheme, the infrastructure of training staff that would be needed to manage it throughout the hospitals and other health care settings in the county, and the funding that would be released by the Training Agency.

This funding was based on the number of trainees entering the scheme and on other performance criteria, such as the range and quality of training given, entry into paid employment, or the take-up of further educational options. The ET scheme would be subject to a comprehensive contract negotiated between the health authority and the TEC, to be managed by the training department and monitored by external quality and fiscal control systems administered by the TEC.

Benefits – from work contribution

Much of the business case centred on the benefits that would be given to the organization through the contribution that trainees would make to the departments in which they were being trained.

Obviously, this work-related assistance would have to be offset against the cost of training and support given to the trainees. There would be disruption in departments whilst internal trainers were identified and trained. Considerable training would need to be given by these ET trainers (as yet not in post) to ensure that the new and demanding requirements of the ET contract were understood by the departmental managers and the supervisors receiving ET trainees.

Benefits – from recruitment

But the most important benefit had to be the opportunity to develop a supply chain of potential employees within the organization. Trainees would be expected to seek employment in the organization towards the end of their training attachment, and the progress they had made during training and their understanding of the way the organization worked, would put them at a distinct advantage when competing for a position against raw recruits.

In the event, the organization was able to employ many hundreds of staff by way of the ET scheme. Many of them gained promotion into management positions and so were able to help incoming ET trainees to follow their example.

Getting the proposal approved

The next stage was to get approval for the proposal from the authority. A major innovation of this nature needed approval at the highest level, and it received it. Reaching the approval stage to go ahead with the project was made very much easier by attending thoroughly to the consultation process, both with significant members in the organization and with those outside in the Training Agency and the trade unions.

Networking with educational institutions

Educational institutions were another external group involved from the outset. They included bodies set up to promote National Vocational Qualifications, such as City and Guilds, Royal Society of Arts, and later the Management Charter Initiative. Part of the Employment Training contract required trainees to undertake training leading to vocational qualification standards, but at the outset of the scheme the organization had not put in place the necessary infrastructure to support this process. Supervisors had to be trained to become qualified workplace trainers and assessors to oversee the training of ET trainees. They also had to be introduced to the emerging vocational training system, because this would be the basis for Employment Training.

In the early 1980s, work-related or vocational training was nowhere near as planned and systematic as it was to later become under the influence of successive national bodies, the latest of which is the Qualifications and Curriculum Authority, established in October 1997. This is responsible for giving advice to the government on the curriculum, assessment and qualifications in schools, colleges and the workplace. It brings together work previously carried through by the Schools Curriculum and Assessment Authority (SCAA) and the National Council for Vocational Qualifications (NCVQ). It was the latter body that had an enormous impact on the way standards of competence were developed throughout the UK.

Opening doors to work-based competence

The requirement to involve supervisors in the NVQ system had a far-reaching effect. Permanent staff in the departments where ET trainees were placed were not slow to recognize the value of the NVQ scheme in improving their on-the-job competence. Soon, more ambitious fulltime employees began to ask their supervisors to introduce them to NVQ based training so that they could improve their ability and employability. The training department took advantage of this unexpected side-effect, and used it as a lever to raise general awareness of the NVQ system widely throughout the organization.

In this way, the organization made NVQs available to its own staff, using the ET scheme as a means to introduce the NVQ procedures through an extensive network of supervisors trained to act as workplace trainers and assessors. This gave the organization a significant competitive advantage over other health care organizations who, at that time, were often finding that their introduction of NVQ schemes was marred by employee apathy and distrust.

Accrediting supervisory training

Partnership in training and development does not apply only to the joint projects that can be formed with government agencies.The importance of developing a strong working collaboration with an institution in the field of supervisory management cannot be overstated.

From the outset, there had been the intention on the part of the training department that supervisors and managers passing through the development programme should receive some form of recognition. In the early days, this took the form of an in-house certificate awarded to candidates at the end of their training. It was quickly seen that employees, brought up in a culture of national qualifications, expected the management development programme to provide them with a qualification that would be recognized wherever they transferred to within other parts of the NHS. This need was expressed by supervisors, and was acted on by the training department as a part of its customer-relations policy.

Finding an accrediting body

The search for an accrediting body for the management development programme led to an extremely fruitful working collaboration between the trainers and an external organization. Agreement in principle was reached with top management and the search began for a professional body to validate the management development programme.

A number of professional bodies were considered before the decision was made to seek accreditation from the Institute for Supervision and Management (ISM). The ISM was founded as a central body to meet the needs of first-line managers and supervisors, and in this respect its remit covered the organization's original training programme. It was therefore decided to ask the ISM to consider the supervisory development programme for approval.

The mission of the Institute for Supervision and Management

The ISM is an important ally to trainers who are taking forward a management development strategy in their organizations. It has a mission that sums up more than 50 years of service to managers and management in these words: 'To be foremost in the promotion of management excellence and development and to enhance individual professional recognition through membership of ISM.'

This aspiration to promote management excellence and development is entirely in keeping with the philosophy of most trainers in health care organizations and of other public service employers who embark on a new strategy to revitalise the way managers are developed. The ISM gives advice and guidance on management development based on experience of best practice in a wide cross-section of organizations, ranging from blue-chip to small and medium companies in all sectors of public and private enterprise.

This expertise is of great value to trainers who want to keep up to date with the continually changing practice of management so that they can incorporate and adapt ideas into their programmes and ensure they remain comprehensive and flexible.

In addition to the mainstream qualifications that have been mentioned, the ISM has a range of competence-based courses leading to the award of NVQs (or their equivalent in Scotland, Scottish Vocational Qualifications) at levels 3, 4 and 5 in management. There are also customer service Vocational Qualifications at levels 2 and 3, and a selection of training-support programmes and the World Class Team Leader qualification.

The three-step ladder of development

The collaboration of the organization with the ISM resulted in the original in-house development programme, based on the action learning approach to problem-solving, being approved and accredited as the Certificate in Supervisory and Management Studies. Later, when programmes had been introduced to cater for aspiring supervisors and more senior middle managers, two more levels of qualification were accredited, as the Introductory Award and the Diploma in Management respectively.

The Introductory course was conducted entirely by means of open-learning materials that were studied by candidates, mainly in their own time. This was cost effective, but the learning requirement meant that regular tutorials had to be given by trainers to introduce each session and to follow up progress made. The topics covered practical aspects of the supervisor's role, and included leadership, resource management, communication, effective presentation, and health and safety.

The Diploma course was conducted as a series of two-day modular sessions on management themes. These were linked to the main purpose of the course, which was to give the candidate the opportunity to conduct a major organizational development project, using other members of the course as action learning colleagues.

In this way, the health authority became the first in the NHS to provide a fully accredited three-tier structure of in-house management development for supervisory grades in all functions.

This pioneering accreditation of in-house management development in the NHS led many more NHS trainers to accredit their programmes through the ISM, greatly extending the influence of this professional body.

Advantages of partnership in training and development

There is significant benefit to be gained from pursuing the search for management excellence in conjunction with an external institution that has the same aim. There are other examples where co-operation with academic institutions will also give trainers the ability to leverage their expertise by sharing resources. Many universities have institutes of health care studies, faculties of management and business schools. These provide good opportunities to set up collaborative networks, and these should be explored to gain advantage for in-house training and development.

This kind of collaboration was set up to provide training materials for the management development programme. By establishing good working relations with the audio and visual department of the local university, it was possible to produce a series of training videos in the areas of recruitment and selection, induction and effective presentation. These were based on real-life, organization-specific scenarios and as such related more closely to the trainees' environment and culture than did many expensive management training videos on the market. These became useful training aids for subsequent course members.

Learning networks

These examples give some flavour of the possibilities that exist for trainers to network to advantage across boundaries. As their range of contacts increases, so will the chance to learn of new ideas that can be adapted to their professional advantage. Also important is the opportunity that networking gives for sharing the benefits of the lessons learned in one's own sphere of experience. Networking for learning is becoming an important activity for managers of all types. This is a useful topic to include in management development programmes, and supervisory programmes in particular should make efforts to introduce course members to the techniques of establishing, maintaining, and optimizing the benefits of using networks consistently.

Accreditation for trainers

The majority of trainers will be aware of the advantages of entering into their own professional development networking arrangements. This can best be achieved by membership of the Institute of Personnel and Development (IPD). Since its creation in 1994, through the amalgamation of the Institute of Personnel Management and the Institute of Training and Development, the IPD has become the largest single organization in the world representing those who specialize in the management and development of people. The IPD has as a key objective the establishment, monitoring and promotion of standards across the spectrum of personnel and training and development. These standards have been cross-referenced against National and Scottish Vocational Qualifications to provide a structure of occupational qualifications appropriate to specialists and generalists in the profession.

Trainers will find these standards important as indicators of the knowledge, skills and application of learning which are needed to ensure their personal competence in their chosen profession. By studying and working to these standards – whether they are members of IPD or not – they will gain similar insights into what is needed to carry out their work effectively as line managers can by using the MCI standards as a guide to best practice. We have talked about this method of self-assessment elsewhere. Perhaps trainers can use it to practise what they teach.

CHAPTER 15

New directions

A well-known and unwelcome after-effect of taking part in a development programme is that it can leave participants confused. During the programme, they will have been deeply involved in an intensive exercise to acquire new knowledge, skills and behaviours in the relative calm of the training centre. They have had time to absorb and reflect on situations and come to conclusions about the kind of approaches they believe would overcome the problems they encounter in their jobs. When they come to practise these ideas back at work, they often find it difficult or even impossible to do.

Managers whose development takes place away from their job return to a working environment which is not always conducive to the spirit of learning they have acquired. They find their colleagues do not share their enthusiasm for the introduction of new ideas, approaches and methods.

Changes imported by the newly trained manager meet with suspicion, particularly if they aim to improve efficiency, for people do not react favourably to the implicit reproach that current practices are not good enough. Attempts to disturb the operational status quo meet with suspicion at best and outright opposition at worst. Change-makers should prepare for this and know how to deal with it.

Dealing with transfer of learning

One way of dealing with the problem of learning transference is to use the action learning project stage to identify the difficulties involved in bringing about new ways of doing things. This means that teams should be regularly led through an active debriefing to bring out the lessons they have learned to achieve change together. Team members can then be encouraged to apply these lessons on their return to work so as to help achieve an environment conducive to change.

These difficulties are always present whenever a change, or the prospect of change, affects an organization. It is immaterial whether the impetus to change comes from outside the organization or from within, as in the situation we are considering. The immediate reaction is for people to go into shock.

Reactions to change

Shock is the natural side-effect of introducing people to change. Inevitably, they assume the change will threaten any sense of coherence and stability they have built up in their lives and their organization. Any change disturbs their comfort zone. Faced with this prospect they react in a predictable way, becoming concerned for themselves and for their ability to maintain their function in the face of the perceived threat to their survival. The response is to go onto the defensive, and they direct their efforts towards thwarting the immediate threat.

Managers and supervisors who introduce changes without first doing something to recognize and deal with these side-effects make it more difficult for themselves to manage the process. They can ease the introduction of changes by first reading the signs and symptoms that affect people when a change is announced. The symptoms are recognizable in the behaviours they provoke in people, and once identified can be managed.

Often the first areas to be affected are interpersonal and intergroup relationships, understandably so because individuals become introspective and concerned about the effects the change will have on themselves. When this happens, the mutual support needed to maintain synergy between individuals and groups disappears. Communications become fragmented, leading to poor joint planning and dormant goal setting. The overall impact is catastrophic for the manager intent on getting the change to work. Faced with these reactions, leadership and decision-making become paralysed and the normal operational structures become chaotic.

These effects can be foreseen and can be minimized by planning remedial action at the beginning of the change process. Remember that the first thing a manager or supervisor generating changes in a department or section has to maintain is the cohesion and co-operation of the team if it is to implement the change effectively.

Projects develop competences

This is an essential management competence, and one that will be brought to the forefront during the project management stage of the development programme. The skills gained then – of how to get the best out of people; clearly communicating a sense of shared purpose; motivating them to want to attain common goals; harnessing their combined energy and committing their resources to the task – are all lessons achieved in the action learning phase. Once they have become a part of the action learner's management style, they are available to the supervisor to improve the management of real-life events.

Lessons learned in the project stage of the development programme show supervisors how to introduce departmental changes to best effect. The project teaches the need for careful and detailed planning to be undertaken if desired outcomes are to be achieved. These lessons are readily transferred to help them work as change agents to transform the workplace into a centre of learning.

Defusing antagonism to change

We have seen how everyone involved in change inevitably reacts defensively to it because they fear the consequences will be unfavourable to themselves. It is logical to recognize the converse to this proposition. Individuals will be less likely to be defensive about change if they know about it in advance and are brought into the planning of it. People need to understand the reason for the change, how it will work, and what is in it for them.

Many of the difficulties that have attended the successive major changes that have been introduced into the NHS in its 50 years of existence have been caused by a neglect to think through and deal with the natural reactions of people. This inability to manage change may be the most powerful argument in favour of a review of the way managers are trained to deal with change.

Success is far more likely to result if the managers introducing changes anticipate the negative reactions of their people, and plan how to counter these before introducing the change. Managers who remember the lessons they learned in managing change in their own action learning project will have a better insight into the feelings and motivation of others. They will be able to help their teams come to terms with the reality of making progress in the modern organization.

Action-based development enhances innovation

Supervisors who have been through an action-focused development programme speak about their self-perception having been altered under the influence of their experience. Follow-up interviews conducted with supervisors some months after attending the programme have found them to be more innovative. They are more willing to experiment creatively to bring about new and improved ways of managing their teams. Their confidence in themselves is heightened through thinking more deeply about their role in management, and considering the greater contribution they will be able to make to the management process.

Something positive happens to them as a result of being involved in the programme.

It is an essential part of the feedback process that this outcome is brought to the attention of senior managers so that they can factor this new, improved management resource into their plans, and give their supervisors more responsibility and freedom to practise their competence. The senior manager has the capacity to markedly influence the future development of the supervisor by creating the environment in which innovations are encouraged.

If the supervisor returns full of enthusiasm and willingness to put into effect some of the ideas that are needed to move the department forward, then the support of the senior manager is essential. The main reason for dissatisfaction amongst supervisors is to find they are not given backing to implement the changes their recent training suggests are needed. This is where the organizational culture can encourage or discourage, sustain or destroy.

Towards empowerment

Organizations with effective management development programmes understand that the hidden potential of their supervisors is being released. Senior managers should capitalize on this understanding by being more willing to allow supervisors the responsibility to try out new ways of managing changes in the workplace. Unfortunately, it is by no means the general rule that supervisors will be given the backing they need to innovate improvements. The prevailing culture in many large, bureaucratic organizations, such as the NHS and local government, continues to be risk-aversive and, as a consequence, the concept of empowerment has yet to be widely embraced.

Empower, according to the *Oxford Dictionary*, is a transitive verb meaning to authorise, license (a person to do). Empowerment allows people to do something they were not allowed to do previously. In the context of the organization, it is taken to mean giving people the right to demonstrate how they can put their ideas into practical effect for the benefit of the organization. Most organizations control this process so tightly that innovation is stifled. People do what they are told; even where a better way is available, they continue with the old one because it is accepted practice and to change it is to risk being a maverick.

Until this attitude is overcome, it will remain as a self-perpetuating prophecy to defeat progress. There can be no progress unless people are able to adapt the present to their idea of the future. George Bernard Shaw suggested that 'all progress depends on the unreasonable man . . . who persists in trying to adapt the world to himself'.

The problem is that most organizations reward reasonableness (by which is meant, compliance) and fail to see the opportunities for growth that can be opened up when the attitude of questioning insight is given free rein, and is followed by action to make new ideas work. Organizations that advocate empowerment – whilst resisting the introduction of new ideas – show by their example that their management is about rigidity and failure, not about freedom and progress.

Getting rid of mental baggage

Many NHS employees carry a good deal of mental baggage about the inflexibility of management. Management is often thought to be negative. Employees are conditioned by the bureaucratic nature of the organization to be unaware of the untapped transforming power that lies within them and is waiting to be released. This is because their managers and supervisors rarely give their staff a chance to demonstrate their latent capacity. This is a state of affairs that a management development programme should aim to overturn, by opening the eyes of course members to the potential they have hitherto been inadequately using, and giving them the confidence to do something positive about it.

Given the kind of organizational conditioning that stifles initiative and innovation, it is not unusual to find that many first-line managers see the process of motivating people as being synonymous with that of manipulating them. This misconception has a negative effect on the way the relationship between managers and staff develops, and needs to be confronted during the training to allow the benefits of good teamwork to emerge as the development programme is carried out.

Supervisors learn how to handle their teams by reflecting on the results they achieved as they worked through their own team project. This learning comes from observing how the actions they took as team members influenced the achievements they gained. Back at work, these insights can be shared with their own employees to help them work more effectively together. So the transference of learning becomes a positive outcome of the supervisor's own development, serving to perpetuate the development of a learning culture in the department by showing how the trained supervisor can use new skills to transform the organization.

Continuing support for learning

The training function can do more to help supervisors improve their management skills after they leave the training programme. By giving them the chance to build on the learning that has already been gained in the programme, they will be able to carry this learning forward. They have learned the ground-rules of continuous development and can now apply this understanding to develop their own self-managed learning system. Supervisors and others can then see that the training and support techniques that were used to help them on the programme are now readily available for them to apply to furthering their own personal development.

The two prime examples are continuing personal and professional development through a system of individual learning achievement, and the practice of mentoring and coaching other members of their teams to improve performance in their jobs. Both of these techniques are perfectly fitted to give supervisors and managers a stake in their own development and, in the case of mentoring, to help them to participate actively in training and coaching the people on whom they closely depend for their own success.

A professional development programme is by definition directed primarily to improving the supervisor's vocational skills, and broadening and deepening knowledge of the art and science of management. It need not be restricted to professional development, however. The underlying purpose of continuing development is to enable people to grow – in the sense of becoming more aware of themselves and the part they have to play in life – and to prepare themselves for the future by learning how to handle their current difficulties.

Continuous personal development is a process by which an individual elects to change from their present self-perception into something more satisfying. It is a disciplined process needing to be planned, implemented and evaluated just like any other management change project. The difference between personal and professional development and most management tasks is that it is entirely self-administered.

Personal development means personal responsibility

It is the individual's responsibility to identify the improvements required to enhance success and then go on to achieve the results that count. In setting personal improvement goals, other people, especially peers and senior managers, can offer useful observations on the areas where the individual could do better.

These insights may come from formal performance appraisals, in which case they are naturally going to call for action, or from comments passed in a less formal setting. Both kinds of feedback are valuable when designing a personal development plan, but neither is essential.

A supervisor who carries out an honest assessment of performance – or as near honest as possible – in the key areas that measure success in the management role, is just as likely to identify where improvement is needed. The added advantage of this introspective analysis is that it supports the reflective phase of the learning cycle, which we have seen is generally under-used. It gives managers the opportunity to reflect on past performance, and to question what personal shortcomings contributed to the results, without having to deal with explicit censure from others, however well meaning this may be. The identified shortcomings become the focus for planning improvements, and work needed to achieve results will be all the more satisfying because the plan will be wholly owned by the doer.

The manager involved in self-development will become adept at recognizing learning opportunities, which are extensively available in the work setting. Learning opportunities include the normal range of activities that are designed specifically for learning, such as course attendance, guided or planned reading of books and journals, and selected use of television and video learning programmes, especially those about management. Increasingly, the Internet will become a source of enquiry for managers needing to access learning.

Grasping learning opportunities

More personal activities can be turned into opportunities to learn. These are the many management tasks that contain the potential to be carried out more effectively. Examples of these might include a negotiation about an employee-relations issue, conducting an interview, running a meeting, or giving a presentation.

Whatever the activity, it will only remain an opportunity for learning if it is approached with the intention of extracting essential lessons from the way it is carried out. So supervisors faced with tricky situations can begin the learning process by carrying out some preliminary examination of the knowledge, skills and attitudes that they have at their disposal. They can judge to what extent they need to improve on these attributes, then mentally consider what they need to do in order to improve. Setting these learning goals provides a yardstick against which improvements have to be made, and gives the supervisor a measure to judge what has to be done to recognize whether improved performance is being achieved. Learning takes place in the unconscious but it needs a conscious act to select a learning opportunity, plan what is to be learned, carry out the activity as a learning process, and reflect on the outcome.

CHAPTER 16

Maintaining momentum

The work done to introduce a management development strategy
has one clear strategic aim. It is to gain competitive advantage for
the organization by improving the capacity, capability and commitment to results of managers at all levels.

Building on capacity, capability, commitment

Undoubtedly, a well-constructed programme can add value to
each of these three managerial qualities. Capacity is improved by
extending the range of skills needed by managers; capability is
increased by ensuring that competence is measured against recognized performance criteria and action is taken to remedy
shortfalls. Commitment comes out of achieving learning goals.

These improvements stem from the efforts made by the manager to acquire new knowledge, skills and behaviours. They are a
direct result of the work done to remedy deficiencies in performance that limit the ability of the manager to reach the level of
optimum performance required in the role.

The need to change the way the manager performs is found
through the process of self-assessment, comparing present performance against a range of elements that form the key components of the job. This is the system used in our management
development programme. It has been found to be extremely
useful for determining where the manager needs to improve,
especially if help is given to coach the manager through the

assessment. A good coach will assist a manager to uncover the facets of performance that need to be improved, help to prioritize them into a logical plan, and identify how to measure the effectiveness of the actions taken to change the pattern.

This is how managers develop capacity and capability in their development programme. But the programme also aims to improve a third key attribute of management, that of motivation. This is a quality that emanates from within the participant. How then does the programme help the manager to become motivated?

Providing the environment for personal growth

The answer to this question turns on how effective the programme is in creating a climate in which motivation can grow. Trainers must concentrate much of their efforts to ensure that the programme generates the right conditions for motivating participants. In this way, they can secure the result that managers will leave the programme, not only with the tools to do their job more effectively but also with the will to use them to change the way they work.

High on the list of factors that will encourage motivation in managers is their own feeling that they have been through a demanding learning programme with credit. No manager who truly participates in the learning opportunities and exercises of the programme should be marked down. Indeed, there is no merit in failing a candidate who has really entered into the spirit of development. If the programme works at all it is because it recognizes that the efforts made to reach the learning goals set for the programme are as much an achievement as is the actual attainment of the goals.

Judging on effort, as much as on results

All members of training programmes are different in their abilities and potential but each can be judged on the degree of effort and commitment that they have put into the pursuit of their goal.

If this means that there will be no failures (in the pejorative sense of the word) in an experiential learning programme that we have described, then this is good for the following reasons.

First, trainers can set the parameters for motivation by making all course members aware at the beginning of the programme that the principal aim is to turn out successes only. If people do the work expected of them, they will be rewarded. Second, trainers and mentors must show by their actions that they are imbued with the desire to reward the efforts made by participants to achieve the aims and purposes of the programme. Trainers should not be in the business of applying petty sanctions to distract adults away from the important task of learning how to become better managers.

There is clear evidence gained from experience that this attitude towards adult learning and development pays dividends. Freed from the unreasonable fear that they will not make the grade, the course members can concentrate on the essentials and enter wholeheartedly into acquiring more effective knowledge, skills and behaviour patterns. Learning can be difficult enough without placing undue obstacles in the way of its attainment.

The response of course members to this more liberal learning regime has vindicated an approach that some may consider is lacking in academic rigour. The fact is that this kind of programme is not designed to turn out academics. It is designed to develop practical exponents of the art and science of management, and research into the long-term achievements of supervisors and other managers who have been stretched in the programme fully justifies this approach.

Ambassadors of learning

Motivation is also encouraged by treating course members as if they are ambassadors for learning, which in effect they are. It is especially important to recognize in this way the pioneers who form the initial intake for a new development programme. They will be under the scrutiny of their peers (especially those who were not successful in gaining a place in that intake), and also of their managers. It is important for them to come out of the programme with credit, to justify the investment in time and resources that has been made in them.

It is also important for the credibility of the development strategy and for the participants' self-esteem that supervisors are seen to give a good account of themselves when they return to work. At the very least, they should be able to be demonstrably more effective in leading their teams to achieve measurable improvements in performance, and do this with greater consistency than was possible before they attended the development programme.

Continuous assessment of the results of training and development

The question of improved supervisory performance needs to be pursued as an ongoing research project to determine the effects of the changes in management practice that course members introduce into the workplace as a result of their training. How are they putting into effect the improvement plans they made during the training course? Where is the evidence that the in-house approach is changing the organization for the better? Learning, as has been said before, comes when theory is put into practice. There needs to be some method of finding out if this follow-through is taking place.

Trainers should be alert to the need to track the progress of course members on a regular basis and over a relatively lengthy timescale, say, one to three years. Tracking can be done using the market research skills used early on when planning the development of the programme. Once again, this is an opportunity for the trainer to get alongside senior managers who sponsored the candidates to examine the progress that has been made to put into effect the learning gained in the programme. It is important that evidence of progress made is shared with the candidate and recognition given for it at the discussion.

Keeping top management informed of progress

It is even more important to maintain the commitment and interest of top management in the development strategy as it unfolds. To this end, the trainer can make sure that evidence of beneficial changes made as a result of the supervisory development programme is communicated to the executive board members and to senior managers.

These regular reports of new methods can be circulated to other parts of the organization, for the purpose of sharing best practice and to encourage it to be taken up elsewhere. These accounts can be consolidated into an account of training and development that should form a part of the organization's annual report.

Maintaining the momentum of training and development is a continuous process. It is useful to have a routine for drawing attention to the achievements of the programme, as well as one for identifying any shortcomings which can then be amended. This is why it is so vital to design and use effective feedback systems to check the effectiveness of the training and development strategy over time. Feedback gives the warts-and-all picture of progress and allows action to be taken to paint out the blemishes so that they do not reappear in later programmes.

Using feedback to promote action

The danger of soliciting feedback lies not in what it reveals, but in not taking action to use it constructively to shape future events. It is stupid to go to the trouble of seeking feedback only to ignore it. Not only will the respondent become aware that nothing has been done, but the recipient of the feedback will be overlooking significant opportunities to make necessary improvements. The lessons that can be learned from feedback are pointers to action and will repay the effort made to implement them.

Suggested reading

Some of these books and journals are mentioned in the text. Other publications in this list have been found useful for encouraging a wide-ranging consideration of many of the issues of interest to trainers and supervisors who are embarking on the joint venture of mutual development.

Belbin, R.M. (1981) *Management Teams.* London: William Heinemann.

Briner, W., Geddes, M. and Hastings, C. (1990) *Project Leadership.* Aldershot: Gower.

Buzan, T. and Buzan, B. (1993) *The Mind Map Book.* London: BBC Books.

Covey, Stephen R. (1992) *The Seven Habits of Highly Effective People.* London: Simon and Schuster.

Covey, Stephen R. and Merrill, A. Roger (1994) *First Things First.* London: Simon and Schuster.

De Bono, Edward (1987) *Six Thinking Hats.* Harmondsworth: Penguin.

Drucker, Peter F. (1968) *The Practice of Management.* London: Pan Books.

Drucker, Peter F. (1977) *Management – an Abridged and Revised Version of Management: Tasks, Responsibilities, Practices.* London: Pan Books.

Drucker, Peter F. (1977) *People and Performance: the Best of Peter Drucker on Management.* London: William Heinemann.

Evans, D. (1999) *Supervisory Management* (fifth edition). London: Cassell.

Griffiths, Roy (1983) *The NHS Management Inquiry* [the Griffiths Report]. London: DHSS.

Handy, C. (1989) *The Age of Unreason.* London: Basic Books.

Honey, P. and Mumford, A. (1986) *A Manual of Learning Styles.* Maidenhead: Honey.

Irvine, A.S. (1970) *Improving Industrial Communication.* London: Industrial Society/Gower.

Kawasaki, G. (1992) *Selling the Dream.* New York: HarperCollins.

Kolb, D.(1984) *Experiential Learning.* Englewood Cliffs: Prentice-Hall.

Margerison, C. (1978) *Influencing Organizational Change.* London: Institute of Personnel Management.

Morris, J. and Burgoyne, J. (1973) *Developing Resourceful Managers.* London: Institute of Personnel Management.

Mumford, A. (1993) *How Managers Can Develop Managers.* Aldershot: Gower.

Revans, R.W. (1978) *The ABC of Action Learning.* Salford: Revans Centre for Action Learning and Research.

Revans, R.W. (1980) *Action Learning.* London: Blond and Briggs.

Revans, R.W. (ed.) (1972) *Hospitals: Communication, Choice, and Change.* London: Tavistock Publications.

Semler, R. (1993) *Maverick, the Success Story behind the World's Most Unusual Workplace.* London: Arrow.

Tichy, N.M. and Devanna, M.A. (1997) *The Transformational Leader: the Key to Global Competitiveness.* New York: John Wiley and Sons.

Worrall, L. and Cary, C. (1998) *The Quality of Working Life: The 1998 Survey of Managers' Changing Experience.* London: Institute of Management.

Useful addresses

Business Links in England
For contact details of the Business Link in your area,
call 0345 567 765

Business Connect is the equivalent service in Wales.
To contact the local office, call 0345 96 97 98

Campaign for Learning
Royal Society of Arts
8 John Adam Street
London WC2 6EZ
Tel: 0171 930 5115
Fax: 0171 930 8556

City and Guilds of London Institute
1 Giltspur Street
London EC1A 9DD
Tel: 0171 294 2468
Fax: 0171 294 2400

Cranfield School of Management
Cranfield
Bedford MK43 0AL
Tel: 01234 751122
Fax: 01234 751 806

Industrial Society
Robert Hyde House
48 Bryanstone Square
London W1N 7LN
Tel: 0171 262 2401
Fax: 0171 723 2007

Institute of Management
Management House
Cottingham Road
Corby
Northants NN17 1TT
Tel: 01536 204 222
Fax: 01536 201 651

Institute of Personnel and Development
IPD House
Camp Road
Wimbledon
London SW19 4UX
Tel: 0181 971 9000
Fax: 0181 263 3333

Institute for Supervision and Management
Stowe House
Netherstowe
Lichfield
Staffs WS13 6TJ
Tel: 01543 251346
Fax: 01543 415804

International Foundation for Action Learning
IFAL Administrator
Department of Management Learning
The Management School
Lancaster University
Lancaster LA1 4YX
Tel/Fax: 01524 812 254

Investors in People UK Ltd (IiP)
4th Floor
7–10 Chandos Street
London W1M 9DE
Tel: 0171 467 1900
Fax: 0171 636 2386

Management Charter Initiative
Russell Square House
10–12 Russell Square
London WC1 5BZ
Tel: 0171 872 9000
Fax: 0171 872 9099

Management and Development Group
Scottish Health Service Centre
Crewe Road South
Edinburgh EH4 2FL
Tel: 0131 332 2335
Fax: 0131 315 2369

National Training Awards Office
Room W825
Moorfoot
Sheffield S1 4PQ
Tel: 0114 259 3419

National Vocational Qualifications
For enquiries, call the enquiry line on 0171 728 1914

NEBS Management
1 Giltspur Street
London EC1A 9DD
Tel: 0171 294 2470
Fax: 0171 294 2402

NHS Development Unit
NHS Executive
Room GN35E
Quarry House
Quarry Hill
Leeds LS2 7UE
Tel: 0113 254 5000
Fax: 0113 254 6127

The Open Learning Foundation Group
3 Devonshire Street
London W1N 2BA
Tel: 0171 636 4186
Fax: 0171 631 0132

The Open University
Milton Keynes
Buckinghamshire MK7 6AA
Tel: 01908 274 066

Qualification and Curriculum Authority
For information on this body, that now incorporates the work previously done by NCVQ and SCAA, contact 0171 229 1234 or write to:
QCA Customer Services
Newcombe House
45 Notting Hill Gate
London W11 3JB

The Revans Centre for Action Learning and Research
Maxwell Building
University of Salford
The Crescent
Salford M5 4WT
Tel: 0161 745 5718
Fax: 0161 745 5999

Index